HOTSHOT

HOTSHOT

THE STORY OF A LITTLE RED DEVIL

MY LIFE AS A FOOTBALL HOOLIGAN LEADER

As told to Colin Blaney

Milo Books Ltd

Published in March 2013 by Milo Books

ISBN 978-1-908479-41-9

Typeset by Jayne Walsh

Printed and bound by
CPI Group (UK) Ltd, Croydon, CR0 4YY

MILO BOOKS LTD
www.milobooks.com

Before you read on, I want to make it clear that the only reason I have used the term 'Munich' to refer to a United supporter is because it's what other teams' fans sometimes called us. It refers to the Munich air disaster and I personally find it disgusting that they should wind us up in this way. I'm not endorsing its use and would never want anyone to think I was.

HOTSHOT

Colin Blaney is also the author of *Grafters: The Inside Story of the Wide Awake Firm, Europe's Most Prolific Sneak Thieves*. See www.colinblaney.co.uk for details.

CONTENTS

Foreword

I first got to know Hotshot while out and about town in the late 80s. I hung around the same places as him and we ended up being friends. He was a character and I'd like to be able to tell you some of the things that I got up to with him – but as I can't remember most of them this is going to be quite short.

Manchester was a good place to be in those days. I used to go to the Thunder Dome in Miles Platting with 'Shot, which was a bit rough but full of good lads. It had a decent atmosphere and everybody was always off their heads. He was a party head, like me, and one of the funniest nights of my life was when he fell down some stairs whilst dancing. My mate, who's about six foot five, picked him up off the floor and 'Shot, who's only around five foot, looked like a little baby being carried up the stairs. He's a good lad and his life makes for an interesting book. Read on and gain an insight into this well-known and well-liked character.

Mark 'Bez' Berry, Happy Mondays

Preface

The first time I came across Hotshot was on August 4, 1987.

It was derby day, and we were deep in the heart of Moss Side, looking for the Blues. As most of you will know, Moss Side has a large Afro-Caribbean population, which meant that we stood out like sore thumbs. All of our firm were white lads, with several boys fresh out of jail at the front, sporting skinheads. We looked as if we were on a National Front march. We usually had a couple of black and mixed-race lads onboard, but on this occasion there wasn't a spot of colour to be seen, which seemed to rub the local Rastas up the wrong way.

'Bumba claat!' yelled an old dread from the doorway of the Claremont pub. 'You'll get what's raas claat comin' to you when you see our bwoys!'

He was referring to City's Young Guvnors mob, many of whom were black.

'Where the fuck are your bumba-raasclaat bad bwoys now den?' I shouted, mimicking the way the old man spoke.

Moss Side was City's manor and there was a match going on, so we knew they'd be about. There was an edge to this pre-season match. It was no friendly.

We were trying to act as if we weren't at all nervous, but we had butterflies in our stomachs and a strong feeling of unease. We were in the heart of enemy territory. Both the game and the accompanying violence would soon be kicking off, because we'd arranged to have it with the 'blue moons' at 7.30.

'Easy now, chaps, keep the pack tight. I can smell blue shite!' shouted Sully, one of the boys from Benchill in Wythenshawe.

HOTSHOT

It was a humid night and you could have cut the tension with a knife. We were all on edge, waiting for City's boys to show.

I took my belt off and wrapped it around my knuckles. A lad called Rabbi from Salford snapped a five-foot steel aerial off a nearby van, ready to use it as a whip. The need to arm ourselves betrayed our true feelings. Although we had gone there looking for it, we still had a bad case of the jitters. We were on the frontline, actively seeking confrontation in a rough-arse ragged area, which was enough to unnerve even the gamest of our lads.

Still, it was a derby day and we had to show the bitter blues who the real guv'nors were. Nothing was going to stop us from giving the cunts a hammering – least of all a bit of nerves.

A tour of City's regular haunts soon reduced our feelings of apprehension as they were nowhere to be seen. A couple of random pissheads were stood around the entrance to their social club, but there was no sign of their boys.

It seemed funny to me. We couldn't have been particularly hard to find. A bunch of white football thugs, walking round a predominantly black estate – you wouldn't exactly have to strain your eyes to notice us, would you?

We bowled over to the Kippax End forecourt to see if there was a mob out for us. There was just one single, huge Afro-head milling around the streets. It was Daft Donald, a former member of the Kool Kats, City's main black firm back in the day.

'Where's the Guvnors? I've not seen any of your lot!' shouted a lad known as the General, United's top boy at the time.

'Wait 'til halftime!' Donald yelled back. 'They'll be here.'

Halftime came and there was still no sign of City. What were these cunts playing at? They had given us a time and place, and then failed to show their faces. We were going to have to hunt them down in their end.

Preface

We poured into the Kippax and sent our younger lads off to suss out where they were. It was like finding the Invisible Man, which was strange because there were only 20,000 in the whole of Maine Road that night and the Kippax alone held well over 30,000. It wasn't as if they had a massive crowd of people to get lost in. They had to be deliberately avoiding us.

After spending the second half of the match fruitlessly hunting for our rivals, we decided to have a walk around their manor. It was our way of taking the piss, of showing them that the whole of Manchester was ours. The locals looked on in astonishment as 30 white Red Devils marched across the parkway onto Doddington Close. This was the stomping ground of the infamous Doddington Gang, whose battles with the rival Gooch Close Crew led to Manchester being labelled 'Gunchester' and the 'Bronx of Britain' soon after. It was a dangerous place to mooch about in, but we were determined not to let the moodiness of our surroundings deter us from our mission.

We headed to the Great Western pub, singing, 'He's here, he's there, he's every fucking where, Brian McClair!', as Choccy had grabbed two of the three goals in our 3-1 win on his debut. Once we'd finished belting out our song outside the boozer, we made our way over to the Pepper Hill for a couple of pints. This pub was directly opposite Moss Side Precinct, strictly Afro-Caribbean territory where even some mixed-race kids weren't welcome. As we piled inside the boozer we began to wish we had our black lads with us.

'Wha'ppen?' shouted the landlord as we bounced through the door. 'Ya lookin' like a pack of bloodclaat bulldogs. Now get away from me yard, me tell ya!'

He loudly sucked his teeth at us, as Jamaicans do when they want you to know they're pissed off.

'Who's making them Skippy the Kangaroo sounds?' blurted Sully, taking the piss.

'Fuck me,' muttered Rabbi. 'We could do with the two Obains here.'

Jerry and Ian Obain were a pair of black frontline fighters whose old man ran a pub called the Talbot on Gooch Close. We had nicknamed this boozer 'Roots', a Manc term for HQ, because it was our base whenever we were in 'The Moss'.

'Let's get ourselves to Mr Obain's battle cruiser then!' shouted Eddie Beef, one of United's Inter City Jibbers firm.

We knew that if City turned up at Roots to have a go at us, all of the local players, grafters and gangsters would back us up – even though we were white. We were friendly with Old Man Obain and, at the end of the day, a personal connection is far more important than sharing the same skin colour. He was a valuable ally, so we set off to his pub to get rat-arsed.

The boozer had Man U memorabilia everywhere: Red Devils ashtrays, carpets, blinds, the lot. It made it the perfect place for us to plot up.

We saw neither head nor tail of City the entire time we were there. We'd been all over Moss Side looking for them and there was hardly any Dibble about, so they had no excuse for their absence. On the plus side, there were a few United play-ers in the pub – Remi Moses, Paul McGrath, Norman White-side – which would never happen nowadays. You wouldn't get Wayne Rooney or Nani drinking down The Moss, they'd be in some posh yuppie hotel in the city centre or the VIP area of an exclusive nightclub.

Whereas the older United lads were content with drinking their pints and talking to the players, the younger element kept nagging us to accompany them to the Cyprus Tavern in town, to see if there were any City in there. My younger brother

Preface

James and his mates were playfully taking the piss, calling me a beer monster and a Collyhurst Cowboy. (Collyhurst, the area I grew up in, was compared to the Wild West as it was a bit on the rough side – but before long we were saying it ourselves.)

I was worried that my brother was out of his league. 'You're old enough to do your own thing,' I said to him, 'but be careful.'

James was still a school kid. He seemed to be under the influence of a really tiny young'un who was giving the others orders. His little friend was clearly the one in charge and came across as completely off his head. This lad had no fear.

Even though we hadn't done the Guvnors, as far as I was concerned we'd still done the business by walking all over their manor. The younger lads were less easily satisfied. They were baying for some bluenose blood and the smallest of the bunch was by far the hungriest for war.

I didn't want James getting hurt, but knew deep down that there was nothing I could do to stop him. 'Here, have this,' I said, handing him the aerial Rabbi had snapped off. At least now he'd have a weapon to defend himself with.

As he walked out the door, towards the taxis he'd booked to take him and his mates to the Cyprus, curiosity got the better of me.

'Who the fuck's that other young 'un?' I asked. 'That Gorton growler who looks like a pit bull on a leash?'

James grinned. 'That's Hotshot,' he told me. 'He's the one who calls the shots.'

This fresh-faced young shot-caller reminded me of Little Dessie from the early 70s – an old-school terrace legend. Hotshot seemed game as fuck and had an aura of leadership around him, which put my mind at rest a little. James was clearly in the company of somebody who knew his stuff. I carried on drinking at Roots, hoping my younger brother was in good hands.

HOTSHOT

This 'Shot fella would be exactly what United's firm needed. He'd fight City's top boys whenever he got the chance and forge a reputation for himself that can never be taken away. The Guvnors had taken over the city centre when he first came on the scene, but he helped to turn the situation back around.

The book that you're about to read was dictated to me by this top United face, who went on to become the leader of the firm other mobs knew as the 'Young Munichs'. It is written from his perspective and all of the views and opinions expressed in it are his.

It is also written in Mancunian – so, for the purposes of those who don't speak the lingo, there is a glossary at the back of the book.

Colin Blaney

1
Welcome to Sunny Gorton

As the blood rushed to my head and the busy hum of the traffic filled my ears, my brain went into hyperdrive, trying to think of a way to escape. I was 14 years old, deep in the heart of enemy territory and dangling above a busy motorway, shitting enough bricks to build a row of terraced housing.

'Just fucking stab me!' I shouted. 'If you're going to do something, then fucking stab me!' Although I wasn't too made up about the prospect of a blade in me, it beat getting thrown into the path of oncoming traffic.

Where were all my boys? We had travelled into Denton for the specific purpose of kicking off with their mob. Everybody knew the score, so why had the rest of the Gorton lot gone off? They'd left me to get killed.

'Give the Gorton gobshite a break,' smirked one of the Denton lads. 'He's had enough now; pull him back up.'

They'd made their point. I breathed a heavy sigh of relief but, at the same time, felt humiliated that the rest of our mob hadn't stood. Gorton lads don't back down – we should have done the cunts!

'You bunch of bastards!' I shouted as I ran towards my mates, who were waiting at a nearby bus stop. 'Why didn't you stay and fight? You really left me in the shit!'

The boys looked at the floor, ashamed they hadn't stuck around.

'Never mind,' I said. 'The bus is here now. Let's get off home. There's nothing more we can do.'

Just as we were walking up the steps, a 40-strong mob of Denton came running out of a nearby boozer, looking to finish what they'd started. The driver cowered behind the steering wheel as a volley of bricks went smashing through the windows of his bus.

'Let's fucking have it!' I shouted, readying myself for a second round of combat. This time there would be no running away. We were trapped inside the bus and had no other option but to stand and fight. Punches and kicks rained down on us as Denton swarmed the vehicle. They were all a good few years older and wanted to cement their victory.

This was my chance to get revenge. Those Denton twats would pay for the way they'd treated me.

By the time the police turned up to put a stop to it, the bus had been completely trashed. We were covered in cuts and bruises and I was still feeling dizzy as fuck from being hung upside down. But at least we'd stood our ground this time. We were cheeky little fuckers who'd rather take a kicking than back down.

Those of you unfamiliar with Gorton's teenage gangs are probably thinking, 'What did you have against the lads from Denton?' And the answer would be nothing. We fought them purely to see who came out on top. They were from a different part of the city, which meant they were our enemies. Manchester was very territorial in those days. Every area had a gang attached to it and Gorton had one of the best firms going. We were known as Gorton the Business – and we really were the fucking business.

Gorton is an area of inner-city Manchester that consists mainly of council housing. It's also the place that made me who I am, thanks in part to its long tradition of gang-related violence. The Gorton Beano Boys were one of the most notorious gangs in the city back when I was a kid. They wore black-and-red-striped tops like Dennis the Menace from *The Beano*, and were always up for a row.

Welcome to Sunny Gorton

I was eight years old when I first came across this gang and I was immediately impressed. They didn't give a fuck who you were – if you came to Gorton looking for a fight, they'd be all too willing to oblige. I wanted to be just like them. They were hard, they were game and they were feared. What was not to like?

My first experience of gang warfare came at ten years old, when I was involved in a run-in with the neighbouring estate. A lot of people think of Gorton as being strictly blue, because City's team was founded by the daughter of a pastor at St Mark's church in West Gorton. What they're forgetting is that former Man Utd player Roger Byrne came from Gorton, by far the best player the area has produced. He was an England regular and our captain at the time the Busby Babes went down in the Munich air disaster.

So Gorton is a historic location for both City and United, containing a mix of Reds and Blues. The Mount Estate, where I grew up, is mostly red but the next estate along is blue. This was a source of constant tension back when I was a kid, leading to countless battles with the bluenoses over their choice of team.

Fighting with the Blues was a means of gaining respect. Okay, some people become involved in violence because they've been mistreated by their parents, but that was never the case with me. I always got on well with my mam and stepdad. I fought to get a name, I fought to show how game I was – but above all else, I fought because I had a genuine love of fighting. Nothing gets your blood flowing like steaming into a rival group of lads. It was a buzz-and-a-half and I enjoyed every single minute of it.

We soon progressed from fighting the other gang in Gorton to fighting with the gangs in surrounding areas. We fought firms from Longsight, Hulme, Openshaw and Moss Side, which are some of the most dangerous parts of the city. Most people would have been terrified at the prospect of walking into those areas and looking for a fight, but we were as cheeky as they come. Nowhere was off limits; we were young but we were game.

Gorton has had gangs ever since the late 1800s, when groups of young thugs known as 'scuttlers' fought with youths from Ancoats, Salford, Openshaw and Miles Platting. The neighbouring area of Longsight was similarly gang-infested, according to this report for the *Manchester Evening News* in 1877: 'On Saturday nights it is quite dangerous for any person to come up or down New Bank Street, Longsight, on account of the rough lads who infest Gray Street and Red Bank Street with weapons.' These weapons consisted of heavy metal belt buckles and steel-tipped clogs, which were similar to the steel-toecapped boots worn by 'bovver boys' during the 1970s. If you went down and got kicked by somebody wearing them, you'd have trouble getting up again.

Fast-forward a century and the Longsight boys could still pull a hefty mob together at a minute's notice. They were known as the Inner Longsight Firm and their manor was just across the road from our estate, making them our biggest rivals. It was a racially mixed area and their firm contained both black and white lads. Half of them were City fans and the other half followed United, so they were 'mixed' in every sense.

One of our most memorable run-ins with the ILF took place when I was 13, on Crowcroft Park, the border between Longsight and Levenshulme. Both sides had equal numbers but our rivals were all tooled up with bats. I had no reservations whatsoever about fighting somebody who was armed – strange as it might seem, I wasn't even scared. When I was that that age, my reputation was the most important thing in the world. It didn't matter how badly injured I got, just so long as I proved I was up for it.

'Come on, let's fuckin' have it!' I shouted as my fist connected with the nearest ILF member's face.

My mates and me soon got the upper hand. Nobody could fuck with Gorton! We had one of the top firms around and the Longsight lot didn't know what hit them. They got beaten black and blue before having it on their toes.

My best friends in the firm were a pair of mixed-race twins called Martin and Robert Gallagher. They had a Scouse mam and a Jamaican dad, which was unusual because Gorton was mostly white at the time. Although 'Paki bashing' was rife during the 80s, as a lot of people had it in for the Asian population in Longsight, nobody really had a problem with Gorton's few black (or partly black) residents. We never saw them as being any different to the whites.

The Gallaghers always had an open house. As they had five sisters and three brothers, I'd have thought their parents had enough to contend with, but their gaff was permanently filled with kids. I was in there all the time, smoking weed with the twins. Martin was one of the funniest people I've met. He was a first-class entertainer and soon became my right-hand man. We did everything together. Whenever the Gorton lads came to blows with a rival firm, you could guarantee that we'd be winding our opponents up and being a pair of right little cunts.

As well as getting into trouble on the estate, Martin and me would also regularly get up to mischief at school. We were the jokers of the pack and kept the rest of the class entertained. This made us Public Enemy Number One in the eyes of our teachers. I remember when I was messing about with my mates and Mr Markman, our religious education teacher, tried to show me up.

'Right, you – stand up!' he told me.

I did as he instructed, wondering what the fuck his problem was.

'I thought I told you to stand up,' he sneered.

I was always conscious of the fact that I was the smallest kid in the class. I didn't have a complex about it – but I didn't like being made fun of either. All of the other pupils were laughing at me and I was starting to get angry.

Then, within the blink of an eye, I grabbed a chair and beat Mr Markman to the ground with it in an uncontrollable fit of rage.

'Have that, you wanker!'

The rest of my classmates cheered as the mouthy fucker hit the deck. I was buzzing off my friends' reactions but, at the same time, physically shaking in anticipation of what my mam would say when she found out what I'd done.

Meanwhile, Martin and another good mate of mine, Kieran, were frantically rubbing chalk from the blackboard all over my head, to make it look as if I'd been hit with a board rubber. 'You can say he came at you and you were defending yourself,' Martin told me.

My friends' attempt to cover up the attack resulted in them getting the exact same punishment as me, which was a trip to the headmaster's office and a three-week suspension. The headmaster rang my parents up and told them what had happened. They gave me a big, long lecture about how I needed to chill out, but understood why I reacted the way I did. My folks would always remain supportive, no matter how badly I behaved. My mam even took my side when I got caught with a blade in class. She didn't approve of it, yet she was still there for me, which is something I'm eternally grateful for.

My friends and me got into so much trouble at school that we were eventually put on a programme called 'alternative curriculum', where we got to choose what subjects we were taught. It was an attempt to prevent the naughty kids from bunking off – although it wasn't entirely successful, because sometimes we'd sign our names on the attendance sheet, stay until we'd had our dinner and then fuck off into Gorton.

Still, I've got to give them credit for trying. The teacher they assigned to us was one of the nicest women I have ever met. She was always giving us cuddles and showing affection, so we started to see her as being like a second mam to us.

But, despite the teacher's efforts to put us on the right path, getting up to mischief remained far more appealing than getting an education. It was little wonder the staff at our school wanted to keep us off the streets, as Gorton was full of vice and crime. It was also notorious for glue sniffing back then. I shared the odd tin with my mates every now and again, but was careful not to develop a habit. I wanted to make something of my life and becoming a baghead was never part of the plan.

Coke was also just starting to do the rounds – although, at £100 a gram, nobody could afford to do it very often. I had my first line at age 13. The Charlie back then was a lot purer than it is today; you didn't have to keep going back to the toilets every ten minutes to top up your buzz, because a single hit could last up to two hours. If I'd had an infinite supply of money then I'd doubtless have taken it all the time – but I didn't, fortunately, so the amount I could use was limited. It was something that I would dabble in once in a blue moon rather than caning it 24/7.

As addictive as sniffing it was, there were far more danger-ous ways of doing cocaine. In 1987, aged 14, I came across the worst way. I was round at a mate's house, wagging off school, when somebody produced a homemade crack pipe and started taking puffs.

'Here y'are, Hotshot, have a lick of this.'

I knew crack was a step up from the glue and normal coke, but figured that I wasn't going to get addicted after just one rock.

'Go on then,' I said. 'Pass it over here.'

As I breathed the thick, white smoke down deep into my lungs, I felt a sudden rush of adrenaline coursing through my body. It was far more intense than the buzz from the coke had been. I was suddenly brimming with energy from head to toe and felt as if I could run around the world without breaking sweat. The rush only lasted for ten minutes though. After that I felt like shit, but, despite its short-lived high and horrible comedown, I was still itching to smoke a second rock.

This is too addictive for me, I thought to myself. *I'll give this stuff a proper wide berth.*

I preferred social drugs anyway. Crack isn't a party drug; it's something that people sit at home and smoke all day on their own. Although I would be lying if I told you I never smoked a rock again, I'd only ever have a lick if it was going round at someone's house. I didn't want to end up getting hooked, so I kept my crack use to a minimum.

In 1986, heroin had hit the estate and the community in the Mount was never the same again. Until that point, smack had only ever been widely available in Moss Side, but when the police raided the dealers' homes, as part of a crackdown on the Gooch and Doddington gangs, it started gradually spreading out across the inner city.

Before we knew it, there was a dealer on every estate and Manchester was in the midst of a major epidemic. Several of my mates became addicted and the burglary rate went through the roof. Some cunt did my mum's gaff over and, although I never found out who was responsible, I had a strong suspicion that it was somebody I knew. What had once been a close-knit, family-orientated estate was slowly filling with distrust.

Welcome to Sunny Gorton

I've lost track of the amount of times that smack has been offered to me but I've always given the exact same response: 'Nah, mate, not for me.'

A couple of my mates gave it a try and ended up getting hooked. It took them decades to get themselves clean, which is another reason why I've never touched the stuff. It has ruined countless lives in Gorton and will no doubt ruin countless more throughout the years to come.

Along with drug abuse and violence, football was the main leisure activity for the kids on the estate. If you didn't turn up at the park on a Sunday for a kick around, you'd get your head kicked in – our passion for footy easily rivalled our passion for fighting. Whether we were playing a game or watching Man U at Old Trafford, we always put our heart and soul into every single match.

The Gallagher twins were constantly by my side. We went everywhere together and whenever she was unable to find them, their mam would say, 'Where's Martin, Robert and Hotshot? I bet they're down the fucking football, causing trouble again. I'll cause trouble for them when they get home!'

I was ten years old when I first went to Old Trafford. United were playing Coventry and I was bristling with excitement all the way to the ground. It was finally time to see my heroes in the flesh.

The older lads continuously plied me with beer throughout the game. Somebody would order ten pints from the barman, pass them back to the rest of us and then fuck off into the crowd without paying. 'To pay is to fail' – that's United's motto. If you can get something for nothing, why part with your cash? I carried on going to the games with a pair of brothers from my estate, Desi and Ricko Flannigan, and soon learnt various different ways of getting things for free.

HOTSHOT

At age 12, my two main interests of fighting and football came together when I witnessed my first row at a match. I was coming out of the stadium after an FA Cup quarter-final game against the Hammers when 70 of United's older lads started going at it with some of West Ham's Inter City Firm. The history of hostility between United and West Ham goes all the way back to 1967, when we won the league and took over Upton Park. They have hated us ever since and I was unfortunate enough to get caught up in the feud.

The ICF had a formidable reputation at the time and had been causing havoc all over the country. Martin and me were determined that they wouldn't add Manchester to their collection of scalps. We ran across to help our older lads and, before we knew it, we were scrapping away with fully-grown blokes. We'd unwittingly wandered into the middle of the action and would probably have been hit by mistake anyway, if we hadn't joined in. Besides, it was the perfect opportunity to prove our dedication to our team.

The action continued all the way up Warwick Road to Manchester city centre. I got put on my arse three times in a row. The third time I went down, I decided not to get back up. Punches and kicks were raining down on me left, right and centre. I figured that the best thing to do would be to curl up in a ball until the situation had calmed down. I was praying that I'd eventually be able to get back on my feet without somebody putting the boot into my head, sending me sprawling across the floor.

Luckily, the Old Bill got a grip of me before I was too badly hurt and hauled me off the ground. It was the first time I'd been in trouble with the police at a game, but it certainly wouldn't be the last. Back in those days though, the Dibble wouldn't bother nicking you. They'd give you a couple of digs and send you on your way, which beat getting a charge sheet any day of the week.

United went on to do West Ham, and we went out and got completely off our heads to celebrate. Not only was it a resounding victory for our firm, it was also a major result for our team. Back in those days United rarely won the League, or did particularly well in Europe, so getting through to the semis was a proper big thing. We'd done ourselves proud both on and off the pitch.

As luck would have it, a film crew had been present during our battle with the Hammers and our performance was immortalised in a Thames TV documentary called *Hooligans*. The programme showed an ICF top boy screaming for the rest of his firm to stand as they ran off down the street, fearing for their lives. It was as funny as fuck!

Now that we'd successfully turned over the dreaded ICF, it was time to test our mettle against the Scousers in the semi-final. Although Everton were by far the best of the Merseyside firms, their neighbours across the park were no walkover. Liverpool had a reputation for using blades and I'd heard they were a naughty firm to have it with. They eventually lost the respect of a lot of other mobs because of their excessive use of knives, but, irrespective of their standing amongst fellow thugs, they definitely had a tasty little mob.

There has always been a big rivalry between Mancs and Scousers. The 'Mickeys' would like to claim that they invented the casual scene, but it's contentious as to who discovered the style first. In the early 1970s, most of the English fans that went abroad were bad pissheads, more concerned with drinking than they were with stealing designer clothing. The only supporters that came back with foreign clobber were the Scouse pickpocket gangs, and these were regarded by a lot of people as the first wave of football casuals.

HOTSHOT

However, in 1977 'Perry boys' came into existence in Manchester. They dressed in drainpipes, Levis, Stan Smiths and Fred Perry tops, and had flick hairstyles. Some would argue that they were the precursors to the casuals, although we didn't start stealing foreign gear until later on that year.

The fact that we both claimed to be the prestigious birthplace of casual culture was one of many factors that fuelled our rivalry. The other thing the Scousers didn't like about us was our battles with the blue-conks. Everton and Liverpool were on fairly good terms with one another, and I think they were always slightly envious of the intensity of the hatred between the two Mancunian firms.

The jealousy that the Mickeys harboured towards us, coupled with the closeness of our two cities, meant that blood was spilled whenever our two teams played. Our semi-final game was shaping up to be just as fearsome as our previous run-ins with these cunts. We were going to show those dirty Scouse scabs a thing or two. We were going to fucking leather 'em and send 'em home bleeding all over their fancy foreign clothes!

2
The Scousers

I was excited about our game against the Mickeys, because I knew that we were guaranteed a fight round their neck of the woods. Goodison Park is a rough old gaff. It's surrounded by a maze of alleyways and back streets and there are plenty of opportunities for a Scouser to jump out with a Stanley and take you by surprise. It's a dangerous place to venture into, which is why I was so made up about the fact that we were going there.

It's also funny going to Liverpool, because loads of women always turn out to shout abuse at you. Sometimes whole Scouse families will line the streets to slag United off.

Game on, I thought to myself. *Those Scouse bastards won't know what's hit 'em.*

On the day of the match, 400 of us jumped on a train to Liverpool, excitedly chattering away to one another about what we were going to do to the Mickeys. The train stopped just before it got to the station, which was frustrating because we were raring to get into them.

'Fuck waiting around 'ere!' one of the lads exclaimed, yanking open the door to our carriage. 'We'd be better off walking into town.'

And with that, we all jumped down onto the track and made our way towards the platforms on foot. Nobody told us to stop. I don't know if there were no staff on the train or they were too afraid to approach us, but we were left to complete the journey into Liverpool by bowling into the station in a huge, inseparable mob.

HOTSHOT

As a mighty army of United marched confidently through the darkness, the police shone torches down the track in an attempt to ascertain our number. They needn't have bothered, because there was nothing that they could do to stop us. They would have needed ten times as many officers to take us on. We walked straight past them without as much as a glance in their direction. Nothing was going to stand between us and the chance to do the Scousers. We had come to get a result.

The minute we left the station, Liverpool were upon us. They had a good 500 lads and they were flashing Stanley knives around. The Mickeys love to show their blades, jumping about the place, waving them at you, but as soon as you run up and bang one of them, they usually go to pieces.

It wasn't the first time I'd come up against a tooled-up mob, because the City lads from Gorton occasionally pulled out blades. The difference was that only one or two of the boys from our rival estate usually packed a weapon, whereas the majority of the Scousers seemed to have something on them. They were the biggest tool merchants going, but that wasn't going to stop us from getting stuck into them. Blades or no blades, we were going to fucking do them!

There were two types of lads that carried knives to a match: those who used them as a fashion accessory and those who were actually willing to cut you with them. A fair few lads would wave a blade around, only to shit themselves and drop it the moment you got up close. The problem was that it was impossible to tell the shitbags from the boys who genuinely wanted to carve somebody up.

This could be a little bit unnerving at times, but when I was with the full United mob nothing like that ever really bothered me. We were all in it together and, if any of our firm were in trouble, the rest of the boys would come running to their aid. We were the invincible Red Army and no amount of tools would prevent us from kicking the fuck out of the Scousers. They were going home beaten, bloody, bruised and broken.

We managed to back the Mickeys all the way up to Goodison Park, although they put up a fair bit of resistance and little firms of Liverpool lads joined their ranks from nearly every street we passed. The police were desperately attempting to keep the situation under control by steaming into our mob and splitting us up into smaller, more manageable groups. We did our best to stay together, knowing that we would be sitting ducks for the Scousers if we got separated from the main body of our firm. They had no chance whatsoever of defeating our entire mob, but a group of ten or 20 lads would be a different matter.

The Old Bill eventually managed to put an end to the chaos and we headed into the stadium, buzzing from how we'd got the upper hand against the Mickeys. The atmosphere in the ground was tense, with Scousers chucking golf balls and tennis balls with nails hammered through them into our end. Back in those days, there was no CCTV at the games so exchanges of missiles were a lot more commonplace. Everything that landed near our lads got lobbed back at our rivals, which only helped to fuel the flames of hatred between our two firms.

It ended up being a 2–2 draw, although the fact that neither team had won did little to defuse the hostility. We had done in the Scousers prior to the game and all that was left for us to do was to cement our victory by giving them another going over.

The Liverpool boys were out in force for us as soon as we got outside the stadium, kicking and punching as if their lives depended on it. They put up a valiant effort, but when United are mobbed up we are unstoppable. We slapped them all the way back to the station and then ran them down the street, before calmly boarding our train back home. They would have to wait until we played them in the second leg of the game to try to salvage what was left of their broken reputation. We came, we saw, we conquered. That was always the case whenever we played away.

The second leg was at Maine Road, which is another moody place to go to. It's in the middle of Moss Side and many a football fan has come a cropper in the myriad gloomy alleyways on the estate next to the ground. Combine the shadiness of the area with a horde of knife-wielding Liverpudlians and you've got a dangerous situation.

But still, despite the very real possibility of getting stabbed or slashed, we were really looking forward to a second round. It was the only thing we talked about in the run-up to the game: we couldn't wait to get stuck in and give the Mickeys another Manc-style doing over.

On the day of the match, we headed into Moss Side in a 200-strong mob to see if we could find any Liverpool lads before the game kicked off. We were wandering about the alleyways when we came across 300 of their top boys, mooching about the streets.

'They're here!' shouted one of our older lads, letting the boys at the back of our mob know it was about to go off. 'Fucking come on then! Let's have it now, you cunts!'

We went straight into the Mickeys, fists and feet flying, to welcome them to our city. I'd like to be able to tell you that I remember every single detail of the fight, but when you're in the heat of battle you don't have time to register what's going on. You're too full of adrenaline. I know we hammered them though – you don't forget a buzz like that.

The Old Bill eventually steamed in with their batons and brought an end to the carnage, but by that stage we'd already put the Scousers on their toes. Now all that was left was for us to get a victory on the pitch and our day would be complete.

The Scousers

We beat the Scousers 2-1, which secured a place in the finals at Wembley. United were pretty shit back then, so the FA Cup was a big deal to us. We were set to play Everton, who were up for the treble, which meant their fans would be gutted if we won. I couldn't wait to see the looks of disappointment on their faces. It would be almost as satisfying as beating their lads to within an inch of their miserable, shitbag lives outside the ground.

We made our way to London the night before the game, excitedly discussing where we would go and what we would get up to. When you're that age, a trip to the capital is the ultimate day out: your chance to knock about somewhere different, to do a bit of exploring. The minute we reached the station, we piled off the train and headed to a pub in Somers Town. The boozer was your typical dirty, scruffy, horrible little Cockney drinking den. It was in the middle of a grim estate of high-rise flats but was only a stone's throw away from Euston station, which is convenient when you're waiting for a rival firm to arrive. It soon became our regular drinking spot whenever we played in London.

Once we were all inside the pub, we ordered round after round, starting the day off how we intended to carry on. We were laughing and joking with each other, discussing what we were going to do to the Scousers, when one of our lads came running into the boozer shouting, 'The fucking Mickeys are here!' It was the moment we had all been waiting for. Our opponents had touched down.

I glanced out of the window and sure enough, a couple of little groups of rival hooligans were making their way towards the pub, in an attempt to take us by surprise. Scousers are like rats: they knock about in twos and threes and the next thing you know, they've all got together and there's a swarm of the fuckers.

'Drink up and let's do 'em!' one of the boys shouted.

Rather than charging down the street into the Mickeys straight away, we marched quietly along the road until they were in spitting distance and then suddenly ran at them. Everton had a lot of little scallies between the ages of 16 and 22, but also a fair few fully-grown men. Some of them looked to be in their late forties or early fifties, but we were little fuckers and didn't think twice about having a pop at lads twice our age. After all, we were United's notorious Red Army, the gamest boys around.

The Mickeys showed no signs of backing down. We fought toe to toe with them for a good five minutes until the Dibble eventually arrived to put an end to our fun. The police had riot vans and dogs with them, so we jibbed off into the estate to avoid getting either nicked or battered. Round one had been a draw but the battle was far from over. The day was still young and we weren't about to let those dirty Scouse wankers get away without a kicking. They would get what was coming to them later in the day.

There were rumours that Everton's County Road Cutters had slashed some of our lads, which made us all the more determined to do them. Real men fight with fists, although nobody had ever told the Mickeys that. The next time we came into contact with them, no amount of Old Bill was going to save them. We would teach them not to be so quick to draw their tools; they were about to get the hammering of their lives.

Once everybody had regrouped and we were satisfied we had our entire firm onboard, we headed off to Wembley to find a pub round there. We managed to sort ourselves out a decent enough place to drink and sat supping pints until it was time to head into the ground.

The atmosphere in the stadium was truly something else. Wembley was meant to have a maximum capacity of 100,000, but Manc and Scouse grafters had donned yellow security jackets and charged people £50 a pop to get in without a brief. These unofficial stewards were eventually arrested, but it was estimated that they must have bumped the attendance up to at least 113,000.

The stands were crowded, boiling hot and proper fucking sweaty, but none of it even registered because the game was so exciting. Kevin Moran got sent off with 12 minutes to go, making him the first person to get a red card at Wembley, but we still managed to win 1-0, with Norman Whiteside scoring the goal.

I was ecstatic. We had plucked success from the jaws of defeat and prevented Everton from winning the treble. Now it was time for us to beat them off the pitch.

The police let both sets of supporters out at the same time, which was a major error of judgement, because the violence erupted almost instantaneously. We were crushed up against our opponents, fighting furiously with them for a good five minutes, with those Scouse wankers getting what they deserved.

The Everton boys eventually had it on their toes, which had us all proper buzzing because they were one of the best firms going. 'Let's get ourselves over to Somers Town for a celebratory drink,' one of the lads suggested. We'd got a result against a pack of wild Scousers and earned ourselves a night of heavy partying, which was exactly what took place.

Our victory over the Mickeys left us desperately craving more. We had sampled what the world of football violence had to offer, and now we wanted to be in the thick of the action whenever it kicked off. I carried on going to the games and I'd always try my hardest to get involved.

There were two sides to United's firm: the pissheads, who would fight if it came to it but preferred to sit in the pub all day, getting wrecked, and the hardcore, battle-orientated element that lived for a row. I was always attracted to the fighters because I'd take a brawl over a piss-up any day of the week. I wanted to be just like them, and so I set out to become one of United's top-tier hooligans.

It would be another three years before I turned my dream into a reality and put together a firm of my own. By that stage, the younger City lads had formed a mob known as the Young Guvnors, who hung around Piccadilly Gardens in Manchester city centre, acting as if they owned the place.

'Those bluenose bastards are in need of sorting out,' I remarked to Martin one day as we knocked about the estate. 'We need to get a younger United mob sorted and fucking do the cunts.'

The Guvnors didn't rule anything. Manchester was the domain of the Red Army and a new generation of hooligans was about to step up to the plate. City's reign was at an end; the Young Munichs had arrived.

3
The Rise of the Red Army Youth

'Munich' is a term used to goad United supporters, referring to the Munich air disaster of February 1958. The Scousers called us 'Munichs' all the way from the 70s into the mid-80s, but soon shut up after the Heysel and Hillsborough disasters. That was when the bitter blue-conk City fans took over. Those envious wankers seemed to think it funny that eight of our players lost their lives that day.

'Oh look, it's the young Munichs!' they'd say whenever they saw our firm. 'Look at this bunch of young Munichs here, trying to be the boys!'

They could call us whatever the fuck they liked, for all I cared. If they wanted to label us as the 'young Munichs', then fuck it, we were the Young Munichs. It was no skin off my nose.

The name Young Munichs was used by us in much the same way as black people use the term 'nigger'. We were transforming a slur, taking away its power and reclaiming it as our own. They could insult our fallen heroes to their heart's content because we still had an infinitely better firm than theirs and no amount of abuse was ever going to alter that.

Rather than having to actively look for lads to join our mob, Martin and me were constantly inundated with requests from people wanting to get onboard. Most of our recruits hailed from Gorton, Moss Side, Longsight, Openshaw or Whitefield. They'd heard about our reputations as fighters during the Gorton the Business days, and knew how game we were. While travelling on the 53 bus from Cheetham Hill to Old Trafford, I'd also become friendly with lads from areas we were once at war with. A lot of them wanted in and so we ended up with 50 handy boys, each of whom was more than capable of taking on the Guvnors.

City had been getting far too big for their boots. They needed taking down a peg. Stories were constantly going round about them attacking lone United supporters at the bus stops near Piccadilly station, which made us eager to teach the cunts a lesson. Anybody can victimise somebody on their own but would they be as brave when faced with equal numbers? *Would they fuck.*

It was hard work fighting the Young Guvnors to begin with, because they had a good 200 lads. There were groups of them all over the city centre whenever I went into town, which meant I always had to watch my back. They were a bunch of liberty-taking shitbags too, only ever getting a result when they were picking off smaller groups.

One of our most intense run-ins with the Young Guvnors took place on a sunny afternoon in a city-centre back street. Thirty of our boys were drinking at a bar when one of City's top lads came bowling over to arrange a fight.

'We'll see you round the corner in ten,' he said. 'You're fucking having it!'

We downed our drinks and headed off to meet our rivals, eager to get stuck in. Our firm that day consisted mostly of lads from inner-city Manchester, with a couple of boys from Droylsden thrown into the mix. We were ready to kick it off the moment that City showed their faces.

'No fucking runners here,' one of the front-liners briefed the other Young Munichs. 'Everybody stands their ground.'

Hooligans are like dominoes; the moment one lad goes, the rest will usually follow.

Sure enough, a load of City's lads came running around the corner a couple of minutes later, bouncing about the streets in typical blue-nose fashion. One of them was carrying a metal newspaper stand and slammed it into the side of the face of a lad we'll call 'T', sending a metallic pinging sound resounding through the streets. It was such a powerful blow that I could almost feel it myself.

Before I had time to shout for the rest of the firm to stand, T had grabbed the stand and went steaming into City's mob with it. They were the Guvnors in name alone; Manchester was our manor and we were going to show our bitter shitbag neighbours who was boss. Fair play to The Shit for having the balls to offer us out in the first place, but they really didn't stand a chance.

'*Munich!*' we shouted. That was our battle cry – if that was what we called ourselves then the Blues would know they could never wind us up with it again. It was the cry that started many an epic row with the Guvnors and helped to rally the lads together, ready for it to go off.

After a brief standoff, City were soon on their toes. This was it – we'd got a result. I was shaking with adrenaline as I chased them down the street. Victory was ours. The Guvnors were no more.

It would have been the perfect ending to the perfect day, had a group of undercover Old Bill not been watching us. The street that we had been rowing on was in the red-light district, which meant it was crawling with Five-O. As we legged it after City, three police vans pulled up and a load of plain-clothes officers jumped out. The next thing I knew, I had my arm twisted up behind my back and I was being manhandled against the wall: 'You have the right to remain silent. Anything you do say can and will be used against you in a court of law.'

We'd been having a huge gang fight in the middle of the day so I wasn't too surprised. Rather than being frightened of getting charged, I was still made up about the fact that we'd leathered City. In fact I was buzzing my tits off in the back of the police van, all the way to the cop shop.

'Nobody tell 'em anything,' I warned my mates as we pulled into the station car park. 'You all know the drill.'

The less you say to the Old Bill, the less chance there is of you incriminating yourself. We 'no commented' the Dibble all the way through our interviews, which seemed to piss them off no end. They were looking at charging us with affray, which carries a maximum sentence of two years. Although I should have been worried about the possibility of getting locked up, our victory over the Guvnors was all I could think about.

If the police had known our two firms had prearranged the fight, they would no doubt have thrown the book at us. They seemed to think it was a racially motivated incident because some of the City lads were black and most of ours were white. Little did they know that the only colour that mattered to us was red.

As I sprawled out on the hard, uncomfortable police cell mattress later on that night, I heard one of the other lads shouting to me from a few doors down, clearly still buzzing about our run-in with the Blues.

'We fucking did those cunts today, didn't we?'

'Yeah mate, we leathered 'em.' I grinned to myself.

We had shown those bitter bluenose twats who ran the gaff. Now all we needed was to somehow avoid being sent to jail.

We were released the following day and told to attend a hearing at the magistrates' court. 'I'm going "not guilty",' I told the boys. I wasn't going to confess to anything unless they had me absolutely bang to rights.

All the other lads agreed there was no point in owning up to having a row if there was still a possibility we could get off. The downside to our reluctance to come clean was that the case was committed to crown court. This meant we had to wait almost a year to find out whether or not we'd be sent down.

Fortunately, by the time we were due for sentencing it was 1989 and they'd just had the Strangeways riots. These were partly caused by overcrowding and the authorities wanted to avoid a repeat performance.

'You should all just change your pleas to guilty,' our solicitor advised us. 'They aren't too keen on locking people up at the moment, so you'll almost certainly get non-custodial sentences.'

That sounded good to me. I didn't mind putting my hands up if it meant not doing bird. After a year of waiting around, wondering how long I was going to get, it was looking as if I wasn't going to jail after all.

I ended up getting a £100 fine and 240 hours of community service, which was the most that they could give you at the time. It beat two years behind bars though. It was also a damn sight easier than the punishment dished out in the days of those bad-arse scuttlers. In the late 1800s, three thieves from the notorious Angel Meadow area were sentenced to a year's hard labour for stealing a vest and a cap. It's a good thing we don't have sentences like that nowadays – I'd have been walking a tread wheel or separating strands of rope for ten hours a day.

They had me painting rowing boats on Gorton Reservoir, which was tedious as fuck. It wasn't very nice having to work for free all Sunday morning after a hectic Saturday night, but I didn't want to risk being given more hours or sent to prison, so I was never tempted to sack it off. No matter how bad a comedown I was on or how hung over I was, I was always at the park bang on time, repaying my debt to society.

Although the majority of our run-ins with the City lads took place on the streets, we would also come to blows with them in a rundown club on Princess Street called the Cyprus

Tavern. The Cyprus was a proper shithole. The toilets were always filled to the top with water and it was the type of place where you could go in clean and come out covered in dirt. Its one redeeming feature was that it played good music. The deejay spun a banging selection of indie tunes that always got us in the mood for a row.

City and United both went to the Cyprus. Whichever firm got in there first would head straight for the backroom. The second mob to arrive would hang about at the front of the bar, with the levels of tension gradually increasing throughout the night. Sometimes a bit of verbal abuse would make it go off; at other times a certain song would come on and we'd think, *Fuck it, this is the perfect tune to row to – let's get into 'em!*

The minute a punch was thrown, that was it: pint pots would fly and people would get knocked to the floor and have their faces danced all over. The action usually spilled out through the doors, our nights there tending to end up in a mass street brawl. It was a crazy, dangerous gaff, more like a Wild West saloon than a club. If you didn't leave the Cyprus covered in somebody else's blood then you hadn't entered into the spirit of the place. It was a hooligan's paradise.

Sometimes we headed off to the Cyprus specifically to have a row. We'd be sitting in the Metropole pub in Beswick and somebody would say, 'Right, let's go down and have it with the blue-conks. Fuck how many of them there are, fuck how many of us, *let's go!*'

I occasionally went in there with only 20 of my mates and ended up taking on an entire roomful of City. It wasn't something we would consciously set out to do, but it did happen and we would always stand our ground. A lot of the time we'd have Kano, Little K and the younger Salford lot with us, who were all as game as fuck.

I first got to know them through drinking in the same pubs

and we soon became good mates. Little K was the joker of the pack, always messing about and having a laugh. Kano was just as sound a lad and could be found on the frontline whenever it went off.

The Guvnors were my favourite mob to have it with. We always knew exactly where they would be and they were always up for it. Although we were battling with them day in and day out, it was a struggle to get the older Red Army lads to acknowledge our good work.

United had a massive firm but, out of roughly 800 lads, a good 300 were drinkers rather than fighters. No disrespect to them because drinking was their buzz, but there was only ever a couple of hundred dedicated brawlers and they were always wary of outsiders. They didn't accept many up-and-comers and were notoriously hard to get in with.

It was time for us to up the stakes to get the recognition we deserved. We were going to have to invade the other teams' ends. That way, the inner circle of the firm couldn't help but sit up and take notice. It was the perfect means of proving ourselves. Fuck taking over the Cyprus – it was time for us to take City's seats and show the older lads the lengths that we were willing to go to uphold the honour of our team.

As we sat in the boozer before the match, hyping ourselves up for what we were about to do, I felt as if we were finally about to earn our stripes. 'Right,' said one of the boys, 'we're fuckin' havin' it. We're not movin' for anyone. This is it – we're going to fuckin' do the cunts!'

We left the pub and headed over to City's end, buzzing with excitement at the prospect of turning them over on their home territory. 'As long as we stay together, we'll be unstoppable,' I geed up the other lads.

Our usual tactic was to remain in one big block for as long as we possibly could because it's always easier to defend yourself when you're with your mates. The moment you get split up, the situation can take a turn for the worse. We were going to stay by each other's sides until we had no other option left but to break formation.

As we strode nonchalantly into City's seats, I felt confident that we were going to stay put. We were heading into the belly of the beast, determined to emerge with our heads held high. Cheeky cunts like us couldn't be told where we could or couldn't go. We went wherever the fuck we pleased.

Shortly after we arrived, a big mob of City came running down to meet us. We had made the mistake of positioning ourselves at the front of the stand, which meant we were exposed to attacks from behind. There were fucking hundreds of the scabs and we found ourselves fighting to stay afloat within a raging sea of blue.

The Old Bill were their usual killjoy selves, escorting the majority of our mob out of the ground. This tipped the situation even further in City's favour. With only 70 lads left, we were going to have a major battle on our hands.

We kicked and punched at our rivals, unwilling to relinquish our position in their stand. The Dibble managed to get the situation under control for a while, but City were determined to reclaim their end and stormed back into us at halftime. We ended up fighting toe to toe with them for a good three minutes – which might not seem like a particularly long time, but feels like an eternity when you're up against unfavourable odds.

The Old Bill eventually swooped in and removed all of our lads from the ground. We were disappointed because we'd wanted to stay and have it, but we'd still achieved what we set out to do. The older United lads saw us coming out of City's end and gave us a look as if to say, *These boys are definitely up for it*. We were on the road to acceptance. It would only be a matter of time before we gained our official Red Army membership.

Going into the other teams' ends soon became a standard part of our routine. We would attempt to take the seats of nearly every club we played, which forced the main United firm to give us the respect we were craving. After seeing us come out of our rivals' ends week in, week out, they finally acknowledged us. We were no longer the new kids on the block – we were established United hooligans.

Now that we had the respect of the older lot, the cohesion within the mob began to increase. Rather than being two completely separate factions, the youth and the main United firm came together as one. I'd managed to work my way up from being a teenage tearaway to gaining a foothold in one of the country's leading mobs. I'd achieved my goal.

4
A City Lad's View

There are always two sides to every story, so it's only fair that I let a Young Guvnor give his opinion on our mob. Andrew 'Little Benny' Bennion is one of the founding members of City's firm. I went to school with him and we've always got on well, despite his choice of team. He granted the space to a United lad to do a piece in City's *Guvnor General* book so I'm returning the favour here:

BENNY

I grew up in Gorton, which was an area that a lot of the main faces on the terraces came from, and my old school, Spurley Hey, produced the highest number of hooligans of any school in Manchester. I went there, Hotshot went there and so did the Gallagher twins. Maybe there was something in the East Manchester water.

The Red Army was the right name for United's firm because they really were a fucking army. Nobody in England could match them for numbers. Their younger mob was held together by between five to ten top faces. Two of these were boys called Mook and Gilly, who have both unfortunately passed away. Then there was the even younger generation, held together by Hotshot and a couple of lads from Longsight and Gorton. Their mob could pull 100 to 150 hooligans from places like Newton Heath, Bury, Salford, Cannock and Lincoln.

We had similar numbers but our firm was more localised. Our lot came from Fallowfield, Moss Side, Gorton, Openshaw and

HOTSHOT

Wythenshawe, which are all in south or east Manchester. We also had a couple of lads from Bradford, Clitheroe and London.

Back in the late 70s and early 80s, the younger City mob began to break away from the older lads, who were in firms called the Kool Kats and Mayne Line. It was an amicable split that came about because we were into thieving and our elders were more interested in drinking. We became one of the first youth firms to gain a reputation in our own right and to develop a unique fashion, consisting of ski hats and coats.

It was a bit harder for United's main young lads to establish themselves, because they got grief off of the older lot for doing their own thing. The fact that they were called the 'Young Munichs' didn't help, as it was a name that some of the longer-serving Red Army members were none too chuffed about. The YMs were in a similar situation to Tottenham, who got stick off their older lads for calling themselves the 'Yids'.

A new name was eventually coined for Hotshot and his firm: the Inter City Jibbers. It was a parody of West Ham's Inter City Firm, who came across all executive-style with their 'Congratulations – You've Just Met the ICF' calling cards. The ICJ's motto was 'To pay is to fail' – which definitely summed up the mentality in the North West at the time.

We had rows week in and week out with the ICJ, sometimes when we weren't even playing United. During the summer lads would pile out of the pubs at closing time and fight it out in the streets, back when they had the 3pm licensing laws. Sometimes there would be groups of up to 150 involved.

Our firm was eventually destroyed by the Greater Manchester Police. We had a total of seven dawn raids, resulting in lads receiving banning orders of up to 15 years apiece. United were only raided once and their case was dropped, which allowed their mob to flourish. Only then were the Reds able to reclaim their 'pride of all Europe, cock of the North' song, as from '84 to '89 the Young Guvnors were the only

A City Lad's View

cocks of the North. Anybody who tells you different is totally clueless

Some people give the credit to (or lay the blame on) Ecstasy for the decline of hooliganism in Manchester. Lads who were banned from attending matches would go to concerts to sell t-shirts, tickets and drugs, which meant that City and United often ended up working side by side with one another. Business is business and both sides grafted the 'little fellas' together. This helped to lessen animosity between the two firms, although our rivalry is as strong as ever and will doubtless continue well into the future.

At the end of the day, I respect lads from both sides who were there during the golden era of football violence. Mancunian hooligans paved the way for Manchester to become 'Madchester'. Remember baggy flares? The terraces of United's Scoreboard End and City's Kippax End had that look down to a tee three years before anywhere else. We were the innovators, never the imitators. Nobody will ever be able to recreate the experiences that lads like Hotshot and me have had, because those were special times. I was privileged to be involved and I dare say United's mob will tell you the same thing. It's just a shame that the Old Bill tore our mob apart.

5
Rich in Paradise

After hearing about all the stuff that I got up to as a kid, you're probably thinking, 'Why did these blokes put themselves through this? Why did they choose to live the way they did?' What with the Scousers trying to slash us whenever we came to their place and the Young Guvnors ambushing us in town, it must be difficult for a straight-goer to understand what attracted us to being football lads. I've already tried to explain why I became involved, but everybody had their own personal reason for becoming a hooligan.

One lad who was always able to sum up his motivation for joining the Red Army was a kid we'll call 'C', from Failsworth. He is one of a number of thugs from over that side that we had on board throughout the years and who always backed his mates, no matter what. Here he tells you why he chose to succumb to the 'English disease':

C

The decision to become part of the United football firm was less a conscious choice than something that happened naturally. There was no initiation ceremony where the older heads voted on the eligibility of potential new recruits. If you were willing to stick by your mates and risk arrest, or even jail, then that was good enough. You would be found out in no time at all if you didn't have what it took, which was the case with many so-called lads over the years.

In some cases, being known as a hooligan set us apart from others in our areas and brought mither our way. Certain people wanted to have a pop at us because of our reputations. What the masses didn't realise is that having a tear-up was only a tiny fraction of what we did. I always saw what we got up to as an extension of support for our team. For most lads in and around Manchester in the 1980s, it was a big deal to go into town — let alone to go to London, Birmingham or Sheffield. Your average youngsters in Gorton would look forward to hanging around the Mount pub or going to Debdale Park at the weekend. Now compare that to us getting the 8am train to Nottingham with 20 or 30 of our pals. It's a world away.

The London trips were always the ones that we looked forward to most. When we were young lads, we always got a buzz out of seeing buildings that had been on TV. Bear in mind that we were only 16 or 17 at the time. The London teams were also guaranteed to have decent-sized mobs waiting for us. We used to try and get to the capital as early as we could: a mail train with a couple of passenger carriages left Manchester for London every Friday night; it took about five hours to get to Euston station, as opposed to the usual two-and-a-half, but it was a piss-easy jib.

There was a boozer called The Lion & Lamb just around the corner from the station, which was open around the clock. It was a magnet for all the local loons and could have passed for the nuthouse out of One Flew Over The Cuckoo's Nest. One night we arrived there at about four in the morning to see a big black guy taking on a small crew of gypsies. He ended up getting slashed across his face.

The tube service started at around half past five, so we'd get on it as soon as it was operating and mooch around in various different areas of the city while the residents were asleep. The opening scene of the film 28 Days Later shows Cillian Murphy waking up to find the whole of London deserted due to a mass exodus: the streets in the film looked very similar to what we encountered.

One of our most memorable journeys to the capital was to see a game against Arsenal. We started our trip from Stockport station because the Hector there always let us pay child's fares. This was around the time when a few of our lads had got into the acid house scene and, on reflection, it was also when the novelty of trips to London had begun to wear a bit thin.

We all decided to neck a type of acid tab called 'purple ohms' just as the train set off, as the prospect of cruising around London in the early dawn whilst tripping seemed a good idea at the time. One of the lads had brought along one of those old-style tape players, with massive buttons you needed all your upper body strength to press down, and insisted on playing F.P.I. Projects' 'Rich in Paradise' over and over again. I can still remember the noise of the tape rewinding every time it was repeated.

The train broke down partway through the trip and all the lights went off. Acid is great when you're in a good place with good people around you, but when you're in the middle of nowhere, in the pitch black with the same song continuously playing, it probably isn't the best environment. In fact it was a fucking nightmare. We eventually rolled into Euston around 7am in full acid comedown mode. This was the last time I was ever going to catch the fucking midnight!

I'd brought a mate with me on the trip who was dying to go to the match with us after hearing of all the stuff we'd got up to in the past. He hadn't really been into the footy previously and the comedown wasn't doing him any favours. We walked past a boozer full of normal Arsenal fans, later that morning, and he decided to attack the pub on his own in full view of the police. He was throwing glasses at a load of old geezers, which left us all gobsmacked. We tried to stop him but it was too late, as the Dibble set two Alsatians on him which ripped his jeans to fuck as he lay struggling on his back. An officer then carted him off for a charge sheet and a tetanus injection. Suffice to say, it was his last midnight trip as well as mine!

Most youngsters tend to hang about in their own area, but hooliganism brought together lads from all over the city. I gained mates in every area of Manchester, as well as other parts of the country – most notably the Cockney Reds, who were a top set of lads. Ask any footy lad from anywhere in Britain and he will tell you that his firm was the funniest/hardest/daftest/gamest going. Well, I'm not about to buck that trend. One thing that a lot of people don't accept is that all hooligans were genuinely passionate supporters of their team. We would be the ones who turned up at home and away, week in week out, no matter where. At moody places like Millwall, Everton, Spurs or West Ham, it would be us who were in the firing line.

The shared experiences that we went through formed a bond between us that has lasted a lifetime. Being thrown into a world inhabited by such an eclectic bunch of people was fascinating for me, and is no doubt the reason that young lads still get involved. What we got up to was a million miles away from the mundane existences of a lot of kids at that time. Would I swap my youth for theirs? Would I fuck! I had the type of adventures most lads my age could only dream about and wouldn't change it for the world.

6
Spurs

London was our favourite destination because we always knew that we were guaranteed a fight. The Cockneys didn't fuck about, especially Tottenham's 'Yid Army'. West Ham may have been a tidy firm for the best part of the 80s, but they had nothing on the Yids. Spurs were easily the best of the southern mobs and remain formidable opponents to this day.

Tottenham's ground was one of the worst places in the country to get to. You had to walk along Tottenham High Road to get to it, which backs onto Broadwater Farm –which became notorious after the murder of PC Keith Blakelock during the riots in '85. Broadwater Farm was then a rough, predominantly black estate filled with ganja-smoking, tam-wearing Rastas. It was also close to where a large proportion of Tottenham's hooligans lived, which meant you had to navigate enemy territory to get to and from the ground.

One of our most fearsome run-ins with the Yids took place the day after I'd finished my suspension for hitting Mr Markman with the chair. I had to go into school in the morning to confirm I'd be going back to class, so I was forced to travel down to London a bit later than the rest of the younger firm. I got the four o'clock train to Euston with a lad called JC who'd just come out of a Young Offenders institute. From there we jibbed the tube to Seven Sisters station and met up with the rest of our mob. I'd been worrying that I'd be unable to find them, so I was relieved to see they were exactly where they told me they were going to be. There were only 30 of us in total, which was a little disappointing because we usually pulled a couple of hundred boys. Still, 30 decent lads is all you ever really need.

'Let's go straight into the ground,' said one of the older lot. 'It's getting late and I want to see the game.'

We did as he suggested and set off, walking down Tottenham High Road in the dark. Other people might have been apprehensive about mooching around somewhere like that at night, but the only thing we really gave a fuck about was getting stuck into the Yids. We knew they'd provide us with a royal rumble and we couldn't wait for it to go off.

We jibbed into the ground by jumping over the stiles and settled down to watch the match, adrenaline pumping in anticipation of a ruck. To be perfectly honest, I can barely remember anything that happened during the game because the events that took place after the final whistle are far more prominent in my mind.

Shortly after leaving White Hart Lane, a hundred-strong mob of Tottenham came running out of the darkness and took us totally by surprise. They were a lot more racially diverse than the majority of other firms I'd encountered, with roughly half of them being black and a couple of Asian and Jewish kids thrown in. They were a mixture of different ages too, although even the youngest lads seemed to have a good few years on us.

We did our best to defend ourselves against the Yids but were outnumbered three to one. Martin and me soon ended up on the floor. I was kicked and jumped upon until I was unconscious, then left sprawled across the road. I could have been booted even more while I was KO'd but, luckily, one of Tottenham's lads showed a bit of decency and picked me up off the ground.

'Cheers for that,' I told him as I roused myself back to consciousness. 'I'll remember this.'

By the time I was ready to re-enter the fray, the Old Bill had arrived on the scene and shoved us into an escort. Tottenham tried their hardest to get past the Five-O but were unable to penetrate the wall of blue and white that surrounded us.

Thank fuck for the police, I thought as we were herded towards the tube. If they hadn't arrived when they did then we'd no doubt have been beaten to within an inch of our lives.

As we boarded the train to Euston, I felt relieved that our ordeal was over but, at the same time, conscious of the fact that Tottenham's mob could strike again at any time. I was covered in bruises from head to toe and hoped I could get home without another doing over.

There was a 40-strong firm of Tottenham waiting for us at our destination, which shattered any optimistic notion that our battle with the Yids was over. I was daunted by the prospect of going at it so soon after being knocked out, but also comforted by the fact that the numbers were a bit more even this time round. Maybe we could turn the situation around and do to them what they'd done to us?

We went straight into the Cockneys, trying our hardest to make up for our earlier defeat. The Yids weren't having any of it and stood their ground, eager for another taste of victory. One of them shot JC in the stomach with a flare gun, sending him flying onto his arse. I'd swapped coats with JC earlier in the day, to confuse the Old Bill, and could only stand and stare as the heat from the flare burnt a hole through the front of my jacket.

Fucking hell! I thought. *If it's scorched a big fuck-off hole like that in my coat then what's it done to JC?*

Luckily my pal was alright. He was a little dazed and looked as if he didn't know what day it was, but it could have been a damn site worse. It was the first time I'd seen a flare gun used and I thought it was a regular gun at first. It shitted me up a bit and made me even more eager to get back to Manchester.

HOTSHOT

After a brief exchange of punches, the Old Bill turned up en masse and escorted us onto our train. I was buzzing that we'd come out of the situation alive because the Yids were on point that night. It was a rush to know that we'd been in such a dangerous situation and lived to tell the tale. Rather than putting me off looking for trouble at the matches, it got me amped up ready for our next big game.

The Tottenham lads were always looking for it and loved a row. Some of the other mobs would sit and wait for us to come to them, but Spurs had no qualms whatsoever about bringing it to our front door. They are one of the few to ever attempt to walk down Warwick Road, which is something that deserves respect because it's a naughty stretch.

Warwick Road is the long, straight route to our ground. It was usually swarming with red barmies, who created the perfect cover for us for us to go to work because they'd often kick off with any rival lads that came along the street. So while the Old Bill were busy dealing with the shirters, we'd be left unhindered to steam into the fray.

I remember when a 300-strong mob of Tottenham came bouncing down the Warwick Road, chanting 'Yiddoes!' at the top of their lungs as if they owned the gaff. One hundred of our top lads beat the living daylights out of them and had them running for their lives. All credit to them for trying it though, because it's more than can be said for City. They've only ever turned up at Old Trafford after matches have started, despite the fact that we've walked to their ground many, many times. We might have fucking terrorised the Yids, but at least they had the balls to try and run the gauntlet. They were willing to venture into the lion's den, so nobody can ever accuse them of shying away from confrontation.

Things were never quite as weighted in our favour when we went up against them in north London though. We might have been invincible at home but it's always more difficult to dominate another firm in an unfamiliar city.

'Galley' is one of the Gallagher brothers – to avoid self-incrimination he's not telling you which! He's had a few close calls with Spurs on their home turf. Here he is to tell you about his most memorable run-ins:

GALLEY

Tottenham were a mob that would bring it to us whether we were playing them on the day or not. Whenever we had a game against a Cockney team, there was always a chance that a firm of Yids would turn up at the station. One time we were in high spirits at London Euston, after a row with Arsenal, when they came bowling up to us as we waited for the train. They looked as if they meant business so we readied ourselves for combat and, within seconds, the entire place had gone off. I went down during the brawl and a bottle came flying through the air, shattering next to me. As I struggled to get up, I sliced myself open quite badly on the glass and got covered in claret. I should have gone to hospital but couldn't really be arsed, so I ran off to the toilet, took my shirt off and wrapped it around the cuts to stem the bleeding. We ended up on our toes because Spurs proved too much for us. Luckily, I wasn't too badly hurt and my hand made a full recovery.

That's not the only time that Tottenham have done well against United on their own manor. I remember another game where we saw one of their boys in an alleyway off Tottenham High Road, chucking bottles and hurling abuse at us. A lad called Lacey managed to catch one of the bottles and threw it back at the Yid, barely missing his head, which spurred the rest of our mob to charge in and do the dirty Spurs bastard some harm.

Seconds after we'd entered the alley, two firms of Tottenham came from either side and blocked both exits. We'd been led into a trap. The

HOTSHOT

Yids had a black firm and a white firm back in those days — one of these mobs was to our right and one to our left. Fuck knows why two different racial groups had sprung up attached to the same team. It wasn't as if the white Tottenham lads were racist — they had a lot of Jews and European immigrants in their firm. I guess the black and mixed-race Yids just tended to stick together.

There must have been 250 Spurs boys altogether but, fortunately for us, they were unwilling to come down the alleyway to fight. I think they were put off by the fact that it was such a tight space. Some of them threw missiles from the back of the pack, but that was about it. They'd led us into a perfectly orchestrated ambush though, so all credit to them for that. We should have seen it coming really, but they took us totally by surprise.

Although the Cockney firms could definitely hold their own when it came to violence, there was an area in which none of the other mobs could ever come anywhere near to us. Hooliganism isn't all kicking people's heads in; there are several different aspects to the culture and we were the masters of the jib. If it wasn't nailed down, we were having it. And even if it was nailed down, we would have a go at snatching it. To pay is to fail — and failures we were not.

7
The Inter City Jibbers

The more we travelled away to places like Tottenham, the more we realised we were going to have to find a way of upping our cash. We were all from working-class backgrounds and couldn't afford to zip up and down the country every other weekend. This is how the criminal aspect of the firm grew to be so big. Football is an expensive pastime: you need a constant supply of beer money, drug money and pie money if you're going to be in the Red Army, not to mention the odd quid stashed away in case you actually end up having to pay your way into the ground. Fortunately, a group of top United grafters known as the Inter City Jibbers was on hand to show me how to make a raise. 'Jibbing' is a piece of Mancunian slang that means getting something for nothing. For a lot of people it's just a word but for these lads it was a way of life.

I'd never really been into nicking things until I gained entry to this side of United's firm. Although Gorton has always had to its fair share of crooks, the world of the professional jibber was something I'd only ever observed from a distance until I came across the ICJ. They were an elite squadron of hardcore pickpockets, sneak thieves and shoplifters who moved from one place to the next, stripping each town of its wealth along the way. This group of skilled money-makers was quick to invite me into the fold, showing me the tricks of the trade and helping me to turn hooliganism into a profitable activity.

Some people thought 'ICJ' was the name of our entire firm, but it was more of a term we used to describe lads who weren't afraid to break the law to earn a crust. It wasn't a mob in its own right, just a byword for United's criminals. The more I knocked about with them, the more I learned about thieving, until my trips away eventually paid for themselves.

One of the many advantages of being part of a mob is that a mass brawl is the perfect distraction for somebody on the graft. While everybody else was attempting to get out of the way of a row, the ICJ would help themselves to whatever it was they wanted. One common tactic for having a shop till over was to deliberately start a fight so that we could jump over the counter and grab the cash. It was like taking candy from a baby.

Another way of making a raise when mobbed up was to walk into a clothes shop and walk out with the stock in plain view of the security. There would be so many of us that nobody would say a thing. There was no such thing as CCTV back then, so you could get away with that type of brazen jibbing a lot more easily. Nowadays, you have to know your stuff to graft a shop. You're recorded everywhere you go, which means you need to plan it out in advance to stand a chance.

If there was a way of making money that was against the law, then the betting was that somebody within the mob was doing it. Whether it was shoplifting, selling drugs or fraud, we funded our life of football, drugs and drink by doing whatever needed to be done.

At age 15, an event took place that changed the way I grafted forever: I took a trip to mainland Europe to see United play Barcelona. It gave me my first taste of jibbing overseas and I've never looked back. I nicked a load of beer and cigs on the ferry over, then spent my whole time in Europe looting the local shops. The shopkeepers on the Continent were a lot less clued up than they were in England, never suspecting a thing until after I'd fucked off with their stuff.

The Inter City Jibbers

From that day onwards, I travelled around Europe whenever I got the chance and grafted my way through Spain, Holland, Switzerland, Germany and Luxembourg. My journeys abroad were like a holiday and a business trip all rolled into one. I'd jib the train to Dover, jib the ferry across to the Continent and then go wherever took my fancy. The 'Dam was like a home away from home to me. There were always lots of scallies from Manchester and Liverpool grafting over there, so there were plenty of English people for us to knock about with. The entire city was filled with drugs, brasses and vice as well.

Rotterdam was at the opposite end of the spectrum. Amsterdam was a vibrant, cosmopolitan city filled with foreign tourists but Holland's second city was rundown and impoverished, with a distinct air of menace. It must have had something going for it though, because when I heard United were playing Barcelona at Rotterdam in the 1991 European Cup Winner's Cup Final, I was determined to attend the game.

I'd been partying hard all weekend and left it until the very last minute to get over. Luckily, a lad called 'G the Jib' had a spare ticket for sale. I sold all of the furniture in my house and handed over the proceeds in return for the brief. My girlfriend at the time went mental, which was understandable given how our home was stripped completely bare from wall to wall. I was praying that I'd be able to earn enough while I was there to make it up to her once I arrived back in the UK.

The coach took a full day-and-a-half to get to Rotterdam, so I told the driver I'd be making my own way back. This caused me no end of problems because I was flat broke and there was no other transport available.

We won the game 2-1, with Mark Hughes scoring both of our goals. Ronald Koeman managed to get a consolation goal for Barcelona but it wasn't enough to prevent us from winning the game. We were the first English team to win a

European competition since our ban in '85, which had me buzzing my tits off.

After the match, I met up with my mate 'C', who had spent the day in Amsterdam taking lots of drugs.

'I'll tell you what,' he said. 'The weed over here isn't half strong! I've got a funny story to tell you about what me and the boys got up to on the way to the 'Dam ...':

C

Maccer, T and yours truly were walking through Rotterdam city centre when we saw a pokey little building with a neon light flashing in the window. 'Cannabis café', it said, which was handy because we were looking for some weed. The café looked like our type of gaff. It was rundown and shady, which is what I like. If you went to Manchester, you wouldn't get a proper feel for the place by drinking in a Wetherspoons; you would have to go to one of the rough-and-ready local pubs. I wanted to absorb the culture of Rotterdam so this grimy little coffee shop was ideal.

There was a menu posted behind the counter listing the various different types of weed on offer. I bought some Double Zero, which is named after the highest ranking in the Moroccan system for classifying the purity of marijuana. It's the purest of the pure, 24-carat ganja.

We were smoking away in the café when a battle-scarred Dutch hooligan came in and started telling us about a run-in with Tottenham during the 80s that he'd had. The more he got into his story, the more wrecked I became. The weed you get in Holland is fucking insane. I felt as if my head was going to explode.

By the time we left the coffee shop, all three of us were completely out of it. We were stumbling about the streets without a clue as to how to get to the station. Our original plan had been to get the train to Amsterdam, take lots of drugs and have a butcher's at the brasses and strip joints. But in the state we were in, it was looking unlikely that we were going to make it round the corner, never mind to another city.

We were scratching our heads, wondering which direction to head off in, when a car pulled up at the side of the road. We assumed it was a taxi and piled into the back, flinging our bags down in the foot well.

'Can you drop us off at the station?' I asked the frightened looking girl in the driver's seat.

She didn't seem to understand what I was saying so I repeated the question. I was wondering what her problem was when a Filipino bloke opened the front door and got into the passenger's seat.

'Eh, what are you playing at, mate?' I said. 'This is our taxi. We were in here first.'

'What do you want?' the Filipino guy asked us, a puzzled look across his kipper.

'We want to go to the train station.'

This guy could speak perfect English. Why was he so confused about a group of lads getting into a cab?

'This girl's taking her driving test. She can't take you there.'

Oh. Maybe that was why he was confused. We weren't in a taxi, we were in a driving instructor's car. No wonder the poor girl looked so terrified; she was probably wondering what the hell was going on.

We sheepishly opened up the door and edged out of the car. The instructor said something to the learner in Dutch and she started giggling to herself. That Double Zero stuff must have given us all brain damage; we couldn't even tell a taxi from a driving instructor's car.

After fruitlessly attempting to flag a taxi down, we eventually managed to hitch a lift to the station with some random black geezer. It was a miracle we made it to the 'Dam, given how fucked we were. We spent the remainder of the day getting even more off our heads, then headed back to Rotterdam to watch the match. The moral of the story is that it's probably not a good idea to smoke ridiculously strong weed if you're trying to find your way somewhere — unless you want to sit in on a Dutch girl's driving test, that is.

HOTSHOT

Once I'd finished pissing myself at C's story, he told me he had no cash left either – which meant we were left with no other option but to jib all the way back home. C had it in his head that there was a ferry going across to Dover at midnight and suggested trying to blag a coach to take us to the port.

'If we can make it there for 12 then we'll be sorted,' he assured me as we traipsed around in the rain, getting soaked from head to toe.

After being turfed out of several different coaches for sneaking on without a ticket, we eventually found a driver who was willing to give us a lift halfway. His coach was full of English journalists who were taking notes and talking into Dictaphones the whole time we were there. We were piss-wet through, drunk and Charlied up, so we stuck out like sore thumbs. We probably couldn't have looked more out of place if we'd tried.

The driver dropped us off at the halfway mark and we jibbed a taxi the remainder of the way. Now all we had to do was jib the ferry back to England and our mission was complete.

Unfortunately, C had been mistaken about the midnight ferry. The port appeared to be deserted. It was pitch black, freezing cold and pissing down with rain; what a night to be left stranded.

We had a little bit of weed left, so we plonked ourselves down in a doorway and started to skin up. The ganja was our only remaining possession; soon we would have nothing.

'What the fuck are we going to do?' I said to C. 'We're in the middle of nowhere and there's nobody about.'

Just as I was beginning to think that we were going to die of hypothermia, I noticed a tall, bearded Dutchman striding across the port towards us. He must have been at least six foot four and looked a bit like Gandalf from *The Lord of the Rings*.

'Can you help us?' I asked the old man. 'We're stuck here without any money and we're freezing our fucking bollocks off.'

'Come with me,' said Gandalf. 'I will get you something warm to drink.'

The massive, bearded Dutchman ushered us into a room and sorted us out a cup of coffee each.

'I have to go back out,' he told us. 'I am worker on the dock. You can stay here out of cold though. You will be better off in here.'

Although it was considerably warmer than it was outside, the room that we were left in still felt like the middle of the Antarctic. We ended up having to rip up cardboard boxes and shove the pieces up our jumpers to keep warm. The following morning we woke up shivering our arses off, wishing we'd stayed at home. Worse still, there didn't appear to be any ferries leaving for the UK.

'Let's see if the old man knows the best way to get back,' I said to C. 'He works here so he must know the score.'

We were hoping Gandalf was going to tell us there was a ferry leaving later on that day. Alas, it was not to be.

'No boats go from here to England today. You need to get boat from Hook of Holland to Harwich Port,' he said. 'It is quickest way of getting there.'

This was just what we fucking needed. We were going to have to jib the train to the Hook of Holland, jib the ferry across to Harwich, jib the train from Harwich to London and then jib the train from London to Manchester Piccadilly. If we didn't get clocked trying to dodge our fares at some point down the line, it would be a fucking miracle.

We managed to jump a taxi to the station and boarded the train to the Hook of Holland, hoping we wouldn't get sussed out by the Hector partway through the trip. I had a go at picking some of the other travellers' pockets to pass the time during the journey, but every time I tried my hand I came away with nothing.

Oh well, I consoled myself. *You can't win 'em all.*

We didn't need the money anyway, as we were safely tucked away in the toilets when the ticket inspector did his rounds, which meant we were able to successfully jib our way to the Hook without spending a bean.

There were a lot of Cockney United fans milling about at the port, waiting for the boat across to Harwich. This worked to our advantage because it's always easier to sneak onto a ferry in the middle of a crowd. We immersed ourselves in the mob and quickly hurried past the ticket inspector before he had a chance to register that we weren't displaying our briefs.

The United fans on the ferry were ballooning, singing daft songs about London. 'Fucking hell,' I said to C, 'I can't be arsed with this. Let's head over to the duty free to see what we can jib.'

I was determined to return to England with something to show for our trip, so I filled my bag with anything and everything the minute I entered the shop. We came away with a load of bottles of perfume, 200 cigs and a couple of crates of Grolsch, which made us happy as Larry because we hadn't had anything to drink all day. We still had a crate left when we got to Harwich so we swaggered casually off the boat with it, acting as if we were just your average pair of straight-goers coming back from abroad.

We had assumed that Harwich was right next to London, but in reality it's actually quite far away. Fucking great! Now we had another lengthy journey to add to the itinerary. Luckily, there were a couple of hooligans from down south on the train so we were able to chat with them to pass the time. One of them was an Arsenal lad called Charlie and the other was a member of Chelsea's Headhunters mob. It was remarkable how much we had in common with them. They were of a similar age to us and liked their Es and their acid, which we were just getting into at the time.

'You can have a cheap night out on trips,' said the Chelsea lad. 'We go out with a tenner, buy some acid and then we're off our heads all night.'

'Are you into acid house?' I asked.

'Yeah,' said Charlie, 'Have you heard of a band called North-side? They're from round your sides somewhere.'

Northside were an indie-rave group that had just come out on Factory Records, the label responsible for Joy Division and the Happy Mondays. Charlie and his mate were into the same music we were; we were as similar as fuck.

We were still talking to the Cockneys when we got off the train in London. As we departed from our carriage and made our way across the platform, Charlie started going on about how hard it was to jib the tube.

'I got nicked for it the other week. They've got undercover police looking out for people without tickets now and everything.'

'Oh right, have they?' I replied, giving the nod to C as I spoke.

All of a sudden, we both leapt over the barriers and sprinted into the part of the station that the tube left from. The look on Charlie's face was priceless. Now all we had to do was get the train to Euston, jib a train to Manchester Piccadilly and our journey would be complete.

We arrived at Euston Station just as an army of screaming 12-year-old girls were coming back from a New Kids on the Block concert. Our only hope of jibbing onto the train would be to blend in with the crowd because there was a load of coppers on the platform, looking to nick fare dodgers. Integrating ourselves into the mob was easier said than done, as it's surprisingly difficult to pull off being a teenage boy-band groupie while holding onto a stolen crate of Grolsch.

''Ey, it was pretty good last night, wasn't it?' I remarked to one of the concertgoers, attempting to look as if I knew her.

'Who are you?' asked her mum. 'What are you trying to do?'

We got another couple of similar comments but still managed to use the mob of girls as a cover, which enabled us to successfully board the train without showing our briefs. We'd made it to the final leg of our journey; if we could manage to avoid the ticket inspector for another couple of hours then our mission would be complete.

We attempted to act as casually as we could while on the rattler, having a buzz with the girls' mums and cracking open the Grolsch. It's never wise to let on to the other passengers that you're on the jib, because there's always a chance that somebody might alert the Hector, but we seemed to be a hit with the mams. I even managed to get a rogan josh (nosh) off one of them in the bogs!

When the inspector finally made his way round to our carriage, C dived in the toilet cubicle and I jumped into the baggage compartment. The fella carried on checking the tickets without suspecting a thing, which was cause for celebration as it meant we'd overcome our final obstacle.

Part of the fun of the jib was seeing how much we could get away with. It was a buzz to know that we could travel hundreds of miles across the Continent without spending a penny. The fact that we hadn't had to buy a ticket meant we'd won. We had started off with nothing and arrived home with some cigarettes, a crate of Grolsch, some perfume and a smile.

Some of the United lads were earning serious money from grafting overseas. Not only were they avoiding forking out for tickets but they were also coming back with stacks of foreign jewellery. These boys were the business – they could steal the shirt from off your back without you realising it had gone.

Many of the top jibbers came from an area called Ardwick

The Inter City Jibbers

Green, which is a mile east of Manchester city centre. Martin's sister lived there so I was round that way a lot. I used to see the thieves bowling around the estate in their expensive clobber, proudly displaying their ill-gotten gains. They all looked the dog's bollocks but one lad in particular was even more impressive than the rest. He always had a big gold chain on, hands full of diamond rings and a stylish flick haircut. The birds fancied him and the lads wanted to be him. I remember looking at him and thinking, *This guy's got it made.*

Martin's sister was a grafter and all the other crooks from the local area would gather round at her house to discuss their latest escapades. One day we were knocking about at her gaff when the lad that we'd seen with all the rings and gold on him came in for a chat. It turned out he was a United hooligan who had made a small fortune picking pockets and thieving from jewellers. His moniker was 'BV the Master Dipper', and he was one of the most skilled thieves in the city. Hearing him describe how he'd earned thousands of pounds by stealthily removing wallets and wads of cash from people's pockets inspired us to up our grafting game.

We wanted to be able to walk about the manor with all the latest gear on and big gemstones gleaming from our wrists like he did. He'd learnt his trade from Irish pickpockets, who are some of the best thieves in the world, and soon incorporated lifting rings and necklaces from shops into his repertoire. Here's the man himself to tell you how a tearaway from Ardwick Green ended up fleecing jewellers all over Europe:

BV
Although I have spent most of my life 'living off the land', as I like to refer to it, I'm not exactly what you would consider to be your stereotypical crook. My mother hails from a fairly elite area of Ireland

71

known as Dún Laoghaire and can't stand burglars, thieves or drugs. She doesn't drink or smoke and she is very anti-crime. So how did I end up choosing a career in jibbing? Well, my introduction to making money came at just 13 years old. I was stood outside the Apollo in Ardwick when a Cockney fella beckoned me over and asked me if I wanted to make a couple of quid. He wanted me to do some ticket touting for him at a Genesis concert.

'What do I have to do?' I asked.

I was still relatively wet behind the ears back then and felt a little apprehensive about doing something that could get me into trouble.

'Get in with the people in the queue. Ask everybody who's lined up if they'll buy an extra two tickets for you if you give them the cash. Come back to me once you've used up all your money and I'll show you where to go from there.'

I had £200 on me and the tickets were £6 each so I was able to buy 33 of them. The gig sold out within the hour, which had the Cockney fella grinning from ear to ear.

'The ticket office is now closed,' he said. 'The new ticket office is where this little lad is standing.'

I didn't even have to speak; the crowd were round me like flies around a pot of jam, snatching the tickets out of my hand as fast as I could dish them out. I made £250 in under half an hour, which was a lot of cash back then. From that day onwards, I travelled all over the country, touting wherever there was a concert or a sporting event. It was to be the start of something special; I had taken my first step to becoming a professional fulltime jibber.

I was 15 when I made the transition from bending the law to breaking it. A couple of my father's friends from Dublin had just moved to the city and I noticed that they always had a fair few bob on them.

'You should come with us one day and we'll show you how to make some cash,' one of them offered.

It was a proposition I was unable to refuse.

The Inter City Jibbers

Dublin is home to some of the best zappers and dippers in the world, both of these words meaning a practitioner of the noble art of picking pockets. My newfound mentors were keeping this proud tradition alive. They showed me all the tricks of the trade and taught me how to manipulate a potential victim into a position where his pockets could be dipped. The easiest way to take somebody's wallet is to get one of your mates to nudge the fella's arm up so that you can reach inside his jacket. This is known as 'chalking' or 'blocking'. You can go out zapping on your own, but it's always better to work as part of a group. I chalked for my mentors until I knew the ropes, then I started to dip myself.

Concerts and football matches are the best places to get wallets; people are always brushing up against one another when they're in a crowd, which makes it harder for them to tell when they're being dipped. The easiest way to get their money is to gently open up their pocket, slip two fingers in, grip whatever is inside and slowly slide it out. It's like taking candy from a baby.

As my confidence as a dipper went from strength to strength, I began to target people in suits and blokes who looked like foreign businessmen as they were usually the ones who carried the largest amounts of cash. One of my most successful grafts was from an African couple in London. They were climbing into a taxi so I rushed across to do the jib before they shut the door.

'Oi, that's mine!' I said, putting on my best cockney accent so they would assume that I was one of the locals. 'You're getting into my cab.'

While the fella was busy taking stock of the situation, I subtly slipped my hand into his side pocket and relieved him of 13 $1000 bills, which had a total value of £9000. They say that 13 is unlucky for some, but it certainly wasn't for me!

'Oh no, wait, I've got the wrong taxi.'

The poor bastard didn't have a clue that anything untoward had taken place. He was probably completely oblivious to the fact that he'd been dipped until he got back home.

You may disapprove of picking people's pockets but there are far worse crimes a person can commit. It wasn't as if I was putting a gun to people's heads and taking their money by force; there were only a handful of occasions when a theft ended in violence, which is what sets the old-school dippers apart from the criminals of today. Nowadays it's all wham, bam, slam, but back in those days it was a matter of being as subtle as possible. The youth of today haven't got a fucking clue. The era of the professional thief is dead.

One of the few occasions when a dipping expedition ended in a row was when I accidentally tried to pick an undercover policeman's pocket at a game against Dundee United. I managed to get a grip of the fella's wallet but he had it on a chain and clocked what I was trying to do.

'Gotcha!' he yelled, as he grabbed hold of my coat in an attempt to prevent me from getting off.

Two of my mates realised I was in trouble and started a ruck with some of the nearby Jocks to cause a distraction. My pals were hoping I would be able to make a run for it during the confusion but the copper was determined to hang on. I was considering parting with my £200 suede jacket in an attempt to get away when a load of uniformed officers came up from the edge of the pitch and slapped the cuffs on me. I was then taken to the nearest police station and questioned by the undercover.

'Do you know who I am?' he asked.

He was in his police uniform and I genuinely didn't recognise him, so I said, 'No idea, mate. When am I getting out?'

'You tried to steal my wallet,' the officer replied.

'I don't know what you're talking about,' I lied. 'I know you caught me in the row, that's it.'

My protestations of innocence fell upon deaf ears because the Old Bill knew exactly what I'd been up to. I was charged with attempted theft and my case was committed to crown court.

For whatever reason, there was a group of Hells Angels in the dock with me on the day of my hearing. This made it look as if my crime was somehow connected to theirs, which didn't make a good impression on the jury.

'Did you or did you not attempt to lift a wallet from the officer's pocket?' the prosecution grilled me.

'How could I have pick-pocketed him in the middle of a blazing row? I was surrounded by other people. How can he be so sure that it was me?'

The Hells Angels started sniggering at the verbal that I was giving, which made it look even more as if I was something to do with them. My dad was gesturing over to me from the gallery, mouthing, 'Get these eejits out of the court'. They were making me look as guilty as could be.

There was a break in the proceedings, so I took the opportunity to warn the bikers not to fuck up my case.

'Listen, you bastards, you better not go back inside that court. Are you trying to get me hung, you longhaired cunts? Get a fucking haircut!' I ranted.

I felt like smacking them all.

I was eventually found guilty, which was entirely the Hells Angels' fault. I usually looked as if butter wouldn't melt in my mouth, but it isn't easy to appear naïve and innocent when you're stood next to a gang of grizzled bikers.

Despite my various run-ins with the law, nothing could ever dissuade me from living a life of crime. I was addicted to the buzz and hooked on making cash. Sneak thefts were another lucrative graft. At age 15, I was travelling all over Europe, getting off with tills and expensive jewellery from the local shops. I was like a secret government agent; nobody ever knew that I was there until it was too late.

It was easy to jib the train to Europe. I would get a coach to London Victoria and buy a cheap ticket called a student Transalpino, which enabled me to travel from Dover to Ostend in Belgium for just £10.50. Then all I would have to do was jump the train to Dover and I could go anywhere in Europe. Other times I would walk into the area where they kept the wagons on the ferry and stow away until I reached the port.

Carrying out sneak thefts was similar to picking pockets in that it was easier to work in pairs. During a graft in Nuremberg in my teens, I got my mate to ask a hotel manager to help him with the cigarette machine whilst I snuck behind the counter and quietly stole the takings from the cashbox. There was a good three grand in there, which I quickly stuffed down my long johns. I always wore long johns underneath my trousers and tucked them into my socks so that it was impossible for anything I dropped down my pants to tumble out the bottom. In some countries, all of the banknotes were worth relatively little. You could end up with piles and piles of them, which made it essential to have a sturdy place to stash your cash.

I was rooting around for the safe when the manager realised that something was amiss and started looking under the side, trying to figure out where I had gone. Rather than attempting to do a runner, I sprung up from behind the counter and yelled, 'I don't feel well. I need a glass of water.'

By this stage, the fella knew that something fishy was going on but he was still unable to put his finger on exactly what it was.

'Let's get out of here,' I whispered to my accomplice as the manager trundled off to fetch a drink.

We hightailed it out of the hotel and got the next train out of town.

One of the main obstacles a grafter has to overcome is fear. I could have easily let my arse go the minute the fella started looking for me and bolted out of the door, but if I had done that then he probably would have called the police. Staying cool under pressure is an essential part of the job. I would often steal expensive jewellery from right under a store assistant's nose, which required putting any thoughts of getting caught firmly to the back of my mind.

I always spoke to the shop staff in an upper-class southern accent whenever I was on the jib. This meant that it was impossible for them to *accurately identify where I was from and provided me with an air of respectability.*

'I'd like to buy a present to take back home to England,' I'd say.

If I was after gold rings, I'd try and subtly hook one up with my little finger whilst I was being shown the selection. If I was looking to get a chain then I would quickly shove one in my mouth whilst trying another on. I became so adept at stashing things in my cheek pouch that I could casually hold a conversation with a trinket in there and nobody would notice any difference in my speech.

I only ever got nicked once abroad for theft, which was for a suspected pick-pocketing of an American tourist in Cologne. I had hidden 18 sovereign coins down my long johns after stealing them from a travel bureau earlier in the day, which would have given the police more than enough rope to hang me with if they had got onto them. Luckily, they failed to find a bean and I got off scot-free, although it was a bit of a close call.

I had another narrow escape in Ireland when heading into a pawnshop with my old man. I went to see what I could get for some chains I jibbed in Switzerland when a load of armed Old Bill showed up. Irish gangster Martin 'The General' Cahill had been all over the news for carrying out a robbery and the police suspected I might have been receiving stolen goods from him.

'Where did you get the gold chains from?' the head officer asked me.

'My girlfriend bought me this one in Switzerland,' I lied, attempting to sound as natural as I possibly could. 'And I bought the other one in Belgium when I was over there selling t-shirts to earn some extra cash.'

I was so convincing with my story that the copper ended up complimenting me. 'Your son is a very respectable boy,' he told my dad. 'He seems like a really nice young man.'

If only he knew the truth.

Part of my ability to convince people that I was a straight-goer hinged around my talent of adopting regional accents. I could speak using the dialect of virtually any city in Britain. A strong Mancunian accent tends to ring alarm bells, so I'd put on a middleclass London one to ensure I passed below the radar. I was always impeccably dressed and groomed, which meant that I was able to come across as a legitimate customer in any shop I wanted to jib.

My favourite accomplice looked even less conspicuous than me. He wore a top-of-the-range Burberry jacket and expensive Kicker shoes, which made him seem as if he had a bit of cash. We were perfect grafting partners because neither of us looked like crooks. Even the Cockneys were impressed with the way we went about our business. A lad from London known as 'Mr B' came round Europe, jibbing with us for a bit, and couldn't wait to get back home so that he could tell his mates how sophisticated our methods were. The current generation haven't got the foggiest. We are the last of a dying breed.

Nowadays Eastern Europeans are the only skilled thieves left, although they lack the subtlety and professionalism of the Inter City Jibbers. They tend to jump all over their victims like monkeys which makes it obvious that they're trying to get a wallet. They are also usually a lot less discerning about what they're willing to rob. I have even heard of Eastern European shoplifting gangs stealing packets of chewing gum and 50-packs of Anadin from Tesco to sell on to an Asian shopkeeper in Moss Side. Doing things like that brings the game on top and makes it harder for the rest of us to do our thing.

The remainder of the modern-day crime world consists of crackheads and smackheads, who are addicted to poisoning their bodies with shit. People who sell drugs are spreading death throughout the streets. I'm not condemning anybody who takes drugs because I have had my fingers in the odd bag of cocaine over the years, but peddling things like that does a lot more harm to society than picking somebody's pocket.

I stopped dipping in '89 when I saw a smackhead rob a pregnant bird at Crow Park in Dublin. Our targets were every shape and size there was, from a six-foot jolly in a suit to a four-foot farmer. We went

The Inter City Jibbers

for anybody who had cash, unlike those miserable scumbags who only ever prey upon the weak. The game has changed completely since I was on the scene and I am now a straight-goer. There is CCTV all over the place, so breaking into a building is like breaking into jail. I would advise the youth of today to join the Army, get a driving job or join the Merchant Navy because the days of the professional thief are well and truly over.

The Inter City Jibbers were the best and most prolific sneak-thieves in Europe. We had an untouchable, military-style operation that was up to the standard of an SAS commando unit. Most of the other firms were nowhere near as organised or professional as the ICJ. The Dublin lads, the Scousers and the Glaswegians were the only other thieves in our league.

We were famous within the criminal world because most other crooks didn't have the bottle to do what we did. It amazed them how quickly and silently we could rob somebody. Our outfit was an elite squadron, netting millions of pounds. Where there was a crowd, we simply couldn't be stopped. I zapped at sporting events all over Britain and Ireland, doing the rugby at Crow Park every year. It was exciting while it lasted, but the era of the grafter is now unfortunately over. It's a shame because we lived the life of Riley. We enjoyed ourselves as much as George Best and had champagne parties in the clubs. Still, I guess all good things eventually come to an end. There's no point carrying on a tradition that has been taken over by scum.

BV was typical of United's top shoplifters and thieves. He never paid for anything and always made sure he returned home with his pockets stuffed with money. There were often just as many earners to be done on British soil. The Continent was easy pickings for our lads, but we would also go out jibbing in our own backyard. Galley, for one, was involved in many a graft on this side of the Channel.

GALLEY

Me and our kid started picking pockets at age 12. I was taught what I was doing by an older family member and learnt the ropes through chalking. I preferred to work within a crowd but had the skill to lift a wallet from somebody on an empty street. Nobody was safe. It soon got to the point where a warning message came over the tannoy whenever I entered the local market, saying, 'Please watch your wallet. A known pickpocket is operating in the area.'

Rival hooligans were an easy group to dip because I could rifle through their pockets while they were knocked out on the floor. It was an added bonus to being involved in a row and meant I usually returned home considerably better off than when I left. The regular supporters were also victims of my lust for cash. A tall, wide lad called Liam acted as my chalk while I dipped the fans during the games. Liam's height and build enabled him to completely obscure what I was doing. He would have been the perfect accomplice if it wasn't for the fact that he was horribly short-sighted. His nickname was 'Can Hardly See 'Em', because he was as blind as a bat.

I would also make a bob or two by selling weed to the other lads at the games. Some of the boys have sold acid as well in the past ... well, sort of. We cut our train tickets up into little orange squares when we were on the way to London and a lad called Clarkey flogged them to the Cockneys as 'orange engines'. Believe it or not, he even had people coming back for more.

There were a lot of different avenues for making money back then. Sometimes we would steal the till from a bar; other times we would have somebody's handbag off. Crime is an addiction.

The Inter City Jibbers

There's nothing like the buzz from going out with nothing and coming back with something. The Red Army had some of the best jibbers in the country, but one lad had a reputation like no other. He was the undisputed thieving champion, the best jibber in town.

The lad that Galley is referring to is Eddie Beef, a legendary figure within the United fraternity. He is known as the King of the Jibbers and has been locked up in nearly every country in Europe. Eddie deserves a chapter all to himself, having had enough adventures overseas to fill a hundred books.

8
The King of the Jibbers

Nobody lives by our firm's motto 'To pay is to fail' to the extent that Eddie Beef does. He lives, breathes, eats and sleeps grafting. I've known him since I was a kid and, in all that time, he has never once worked an honest job. He is a free spirit who lives completely 'off the land' and steals everything he needs to survive. Eddie is one of the top dogs of United's thieving element. Here he tells you about his long and colourful criminal history:

EDDIE
Jibbing has been a way of life for me for as long as I can remember. I was stealing coal from the coalman and milk from the milkman at the tender age of five to bring back to my mam. My sister would distract the deliverymen whilst I snuck round the back of their vans and relieved them of their wares.

At age seven, I started going to see United with a group of lads from Gorton, Ancoats, Newton Heath, Miles Platting and Longsight. The boys I watched the matches with went on to become my regular accomplices whenever I went out grafting. We started off jibbing pies and packets of crisps from the café at Old Trafford, soon progressing to picking people's pockets and stealing change from the wishing well at Belle Vue.

Belle Vue amusement park was an inner-city funfair with its own speedway track, wrestling ring and zoo. It was like a home away from home for us because there was always plenty of money to be made from the visitors. Sometimes we would offer to sell programmes for the people that organised the speedway and then fuck off home before they asked us for the cash. Other days we stuck to lifting wallets.

The midnight train to London was another good source of cash. It didn't arrive at its destination until four in the morning and had carriages with beds in them so that people could sleep. We used to pull the carriage doors open, tiptoe into the room and dip the passengers while they were zonked out.

The funniest thing we ever grafted on the midnight was a government minister's trousers. We were on the way to Chelsea when we stumbled across the minister lying asleep with nothing on in one of the cabins. I've heard about people sleeping naked but doing it on public transport is taking the piss. We stole his briefcase and his pants and then crept back off down the train.

The briefcase was full of House of Commons papers, which immediately rang alarm bells. We knew we'd be in a lot of trouble if anybody got onto the fact we'd stolen them so one of the lads threw them out at Dunstable and another chucked the trousers out at Luton. The only thing that we hung onto was the £150 we'd lifted from the geezer's wallet.

When the train arrived at Euston, our unfortunate victim was forced to leave the carriage with a British Rail towel wrapped around his body as we pissed ourselves with laughter. What was even funnier was the fact that next week's papers speculated that the IRA might have stolen the documents: '100mph Sneak Thief Has Government Minister's Trousers' read one of the headlines. We were so adept at what we did that the media assumed it must have been the work of terrorists. The ICJ were grafters with the stealth and professionalism of Irish paramilitaries. The trouser-stealing incident was later immortalised in my interview for Cass Pennant's Top Boys and the entire firm were in stitches when they read it.

There was a failsafe method for getting off if I ever got caught thieving on the rattler. I always had a snide passport on hand so that I could give the Old Bill a fake name. Back in those days it was easy

The King of the Jibbers

to get a passport in somebody else's name. All you had to do was take your mate's birth certificate and a photograph of yourself down to the local post office. Passports needed renewing on a yearly basis, rather than lasting ten years like today, which meant that nobody was ever suspicious of people getting a new one made up. The only downside to using my mates' names was it meant they always got accused of things I had done. They never once dropped me in it though, because friends don't grass each other up.

At age 15, I decided to join the lads on an overseas jibbing trip to Ostend in Belgium. You could jib your way from Manchester to anywhere in Europe without paying a thing back then. All you had to do was jump the train to London, jump the train from London to Dover and then rush onto the ferry in the middle of a crowd. The inspectors didn't check the tickets as thoroughly as they do today, now that there's a more serious kind of terrorism about.

Once we realised how easy it was to graft on the Continent, we went back all the time. My favourite place to jib was Switzerland. The people there were stupid and often left their money lying around; it was also home to numerous expensive jewellery shops, which had pound signs flashing up before my eyes. I knew a fence in Amsterdam who placed orders with me, so I was able get rid of as much Swiss gold as I could rob.

We used Amsterdam as our base whenever we were in Europe because all of the lads smoked weed and it's legal to skin up over there. I always got on well with the Dutch because they had a similar culture to the Mancs. They were into acid house, which was the in thing back home at the time, and spoke perfect English.

Germany was another good location to go jibbing because you could use 5p coins in place of Deustchmarks in the cig machines. This provided us with plenty of cheap smokes to sell when we arrived back home.

The land of sauerkraut and bratwurst was also one of the many countries where I ended up doing a sentence. I stabbed a shop assistant

85

there with his own knife, which landed me in the nick. The assistant had realised I was robbing his stock and attempted to do me in, dropping his blade during the struggle. He'd been trying to cut me with it so I'd no qualms whatsoever about doing the same to him. I ended up serving nine months in Cologne prison, which seemed to contain every nationality under the sun. There were Portuguese, Czechoslovakians, Belgians, French, Chinese, you name it. This meant that I wasn't the only one who was unable to speak the language, which was good, but I was still a bit pissed off that I had to spend my eighteenth birthday behind bars.

On the day of my release, the German Old Bill confiscated my passport because they had sussed it was a fake. I had to go to Düsseldorf to get a special 24-hour pass to get back home. I got the ferry across to Dover and was just stepping off the boat when the plod came rushing over, accusing me of stealing a pack of Woodbines from the duty free. This was bollocks because I'd actually paid for them, but the original purpose of my trip to Germany had been to avoid getting recaptured on the run from borstal, so I was in trouble anyway. I'd been caught doing over the bingo hall on Mount Road in Gorton and should have been partway through a bit of bird for burglary.

Rather than shipping me straight off back to Wigan borstal, the authorities shifted me from prison to prison, getting closer to the institution that I'd originally escaped from with each move. I started off in Canterbury prison and did a lengthy tour of the penal system, visiting such exotic locations as Wormwood Scrubs, Leicester prison and Winson Green. It took six full weeks to get me back to the borstal, which was a waste of everybody's time because I cut the fence and escaped again.

I was on the run for just under two years before the Old Bill finally caught up with me. I was on my way to an away game against Tottenham when somebody put a jeweller's window through and I got nicked for it afterwards. The Dibble soon worked out that I was an escapee and sent me back to Wigan. I was nearly

The King of the Jibbers

20 by this stage and thought, *fuck it, I might as well get it over and done with.* Once I had done my time, I would no longer have anything hanging over me and would be able to walk the streets without fear of arrest.

Unfortunately I ended up punching some big Irish fella at the chippy on Mount Road two weeks after being released. Despite the fact that he'd kicked off on me first, my so-called victim grassed me up and I was landed with another four months inside. You'd have thought that serving three consecutive sentences would put me off breaking the law but when you live illegally you have to expect to go to prison every now and again. I've since done time in more countries than most people can name. None of them were half as bad as the gaff I ended up in Thailand though. The stint I did in there was like ten sentences in one.

The bizarre thing about my brief stay in a Thai prison was that I wasn't even on the jib when I got nicked. I'd been on holiday and got arrested at the airport for overstaying my visa by eight hours. The Thais are very strict on overstays; I'd advise anybody who ever visits their country to return home on the dot or risk being banged up in a grim third-world jailhouse.

I was locked up in a cell with 70 other prisoners. My hands and feet were chained together and my head and balls were shaved to stop me getting lice. *Fuck me,* I thought to myself, *this is some seriously heavy shit.*

The worst part about doing time in Thailand is that they hardly give you any food unless you pay for extra scran. I got an eggcup full of rice brought round every morning at seven, which had to last all day. If I'd been arrested for committing a crime then I'd have at least been sent down with my earnings. As it was, I ended up losing six stone of my body weight and thinking I was going to die. Luckily the British embassy came to visit four months into my stint and told me I'd be released if I could pay a £3,500 fine. I managed to get in contact with my sister and she sent across the cash.

HOTSHOT

The Thai authorities are cheeky fuckers. They didn't even pay for my ticket home, which meant my sister was left to foot the bill again. The plane to England stopped at Abu Dhabi airport in the United Arab Emirates, so I lifted some cigarettes from a duty free shop between flights.

Horrific as it was, my Thai prison experience didn't put me off jibbing abroad. I was still the king of the jibbers – the only difference being that the king was now skinny and dishevelled. There isn't a prison in the world that will stop me making money through theft. It's been my lifelong career and I will no doubt carry on well into the future.

Eddie is definitely one of a kind; he was jetting back to another holiday in Thailand within a couple of months of getting out. There aren't too many people who would return to a country where they've had an experience like that. I guess it takes a lot more than a Thai prison to break a master thief like him. He is 100 percent committed to the art of jibbing, which is something that no amount of overcrowding and starvation will ever change.

9
More Terrace Legends

United's mob had no shortage of characters. We had lads who were like something from a Dickens novel. Eddie Beef's antics overseas will no doubt blow the mind of the average straight-goer, but our firm was full of equally memorable faces. Every lad added a unique ingredient to the mix – even the small handful who didn't actually support United.

We had a policy of never firming up with anyone, but would occasionally allow somebody from a rival mob to go to matches with us if they'd earned our respect. One such lad was a terrace legend known as Millwall Mick. He might not have followed our team but he proved his loyalty to our firm. As far as we were concerned, he was one of the boys.

Every time we got the train to London Euston in the mid-80s we saw Mick, hanging around the station. He was black, had a shiny gold tooth and dressed like a skinhead, which made him immediately identifiable as a football lad because a lot of skins were into hooliganism at the time. We eventually tired of wondering what he was doing there and fronted him up.

'Your game's up,' one of the boys told him. 'We know you're scouting for someone. Which team are you with?'

'I'm Millwall,' Mick calmly replied. 'You've got it all wrong though; I want to get in with you lads. You seem to be getting a lot of action at the moment and I want in on it.'

In ordinary circumstances we'd have told anybody who asked to join up with us to fuck off. But he showed no fear whatsoever, despite being on his own, so we figured he must be game.

'All right, you can tag along,' I said. 'You've got some balls being here on your Jack Jones.'

From that day onwards, Mick was one of the lads. He was a handy fucker and loved to have a row. I remember when we ambushed a firm of Mickeys outside Euston station and he threw wild uppercuts at the stragglers as they ran away. The Scousers were scared half to death and looked as if they'd do anything to avoid this crazy Cockney thug. That day really sticks in my head because, when the Old Bill eventually turned up to separate us, they almost stuck Robert Gallagher in with the Scousers by mistake. The Mickeys actually tried to convince the Dibble that he was part of their crew – if they'd succeeded then he probably wouldn't be here today.

In 1990, Mick disappeared off the face of the earth. We'd just had the dawn raids and a lot of lads had been banned, so maybe he decided to call it a day because of that. Whatever the reason for his sudden departure, we lost a valuable member of our firm. He was always up for it; no matter what, he always stood his ground.

Millwall Mick wasn't the only memorable face I met during the mid-80s. It was during this period that one of the pickpockets from Ardwick introduced me to a black lad called Coco. He was living on the next road from Galley's sister, making a living buying and selling stolen jewellery and electrical equipment. My first impression of him was that he was a 'Mr Big' character, because he was turned out in all the latest gear and seemed connected with all the main thieves. You could tell he had money just by looking at him.

Coco also had a fearsome reputation as a hooligan, putting in work on the terraces since the 70s. Not many people who were good in a mass brawl could fight one-on-one, but he was just as good at scrapping with a single opponent as he was at mob combat. He was as hard as they come but he was proper humble, never talking down to anyone. I was impressed by both his status and his humility, and he soon became another figure that I looked up to.

This Red Army legend's involvement in football violence stretches all the way back to when he ran away from approved school to go to games as a kid. His introduction to our mob came via a United firm called the Collyhurst Crew, who met him en route to Millwall. The football special usually held around 900 people, but this time there were only 400 – not a large amount to take to The Den. Our lads were impressed that such a young kid was travelling down alone, and so they took him under their wing. Here's Coco to tell you about his time with the firm:

COCO
My first meeting with the Collyhurst Crew was on a day when I really needed their company. The Den was a moody place to go to and I didn't fancy heading there alone. Unfortunately, by the time they reached the ground I'd managed to lose them, which didn't bode too well. Quite a few United fans got battered during the match and even more were picked off afterwards. All of the Millwall fans were in their thirties and forties, which was very intimidating. I was only around 13 and didn't fancy the prospect of going up against a hulking great beer monster. I was relieved when I made it back to Euston in one piece and saw the Collyhurst lot waiting for me. They told me to stick with them at any games I went to in future. From that day onwards I was classed as a member of their firm, despite not being from Collyhurst myself.

I've been involved in many an epic battle over the years, but perhaps my most memorable tear-up was after a game against Chelsea in the late 70s. Their place could be just as intimidating as The Den because we had a bitter rivalry with them at the time, starting when we went over to Saint Etienne for the Cup Winners Cup in '77. The Chelsea boys were jealous of the trouble we caused while we were there and wanted to show they could compete with the big boys. They even had the bollocks to let us know that they were planning to travel to Manchester mob-handed to kick off. Nobody had come firmed up to our place without police escorts since Glasgow Rangers in 1974, so they were going to have their work cut out for them.

Despite our high hopes, the Chelsea boys ended up getting escorted all the way from Old Trafford Metrolink station to the scoreboard entrances on the main forecourt. There wasn't much trouble after the match either, as the Dibble kept the away fans inside for an extra quarter of an hour. They treated the game as if it was a test of their capabilities and went all out to prevent anything from going off.

Although there were no brawls directly outside the ground, Chelsea's thugs did manage to get a row at the Royal Thorn pub in Wythenshawe. The lads they went at it with weren't even hooligans, but gangsters, grafters and thugs from the surrounding areas. The incident was all over the newspapers, with reports of numerous casualties in the local hospitals and large amounts of boys from both sides ending up in court. When the trials ended and people started getting sent down, Strangeways jail was said to be at bursting point from the amount of lads who were banged up.

Chelsea had come to Manchester looking for aggro, which meant we had to return the favour. We couldn't have them thinking we'd been outdone, so we arranged a turnout for our next away game at their place. The problem was that United fans had been banned from all away games after trashing Norwich's ground: we'd demolished the walls of their Barclays Stand, set fire to the outside fence and pelted the Old Bill with pieces of slate. The entire incident was caught on camera, leading the media to label it as 'the worst riot ever seen in Norwich'. It wasn't just the police and the Norwich boys who suffered injuries either: one of our lads fell through the roof of the stadium during the chaos and nearly came a cropper. I think he'd have been a lot worse off if it wasn't for the width of his flares, as they seemed to act like parachutes.

We were warned to stay at home by the Old Bill, but if somebody tells you not to do something then you automatically want to do it. The Dibble were determined to uphold the ban and wouldn't allow us on the platform to get our train, but if they thought they could thwart our plans that easily they had another think coming. We weren't going to be put off by a vanload of OB milling around the station; we were going to do whatever it took to bring it to the Cockneys.

A couple of lads had their own cars but there wasn't enough room in them for us all, so I rang up my mate's dad who ran his own vehicle hire business. 'There's a load of people here who want to go to the match,' I told him. 'They're willing to pay £5 each if you can bring a minibus round, which should make it more than worth your while.'

The only thing he had available was this huge box furniture van. He said he would drive it over to us if we could collect a 'long 'un', which is Manc slang for £100. There were 40 of us there, which meant only 20 people would need to shell out their fiver. It seemed as if we were heading off to London after all.

To say it was comfortable in the van would be the equivalent to saying a Mickey enjoys a Woolyback's company (to a Scouser, that's everyone who isn't from Liverpool). Everybody flew from one side to the other whenever we turned a corner. We were falling into each other every couple of minutes and pissing ourselves with laughter. It was entertaining as fuck but we couldn't travel all the way to the game like that. Somebody eventually decided we should sack the box van off and get a train from Deansgate station, where there would be less Old Bill about. The lads with their own cars followed us there, which gave us a total of 70 heads.

We had to change at Stockport to get the rattler to Euston, which meant we had a short wait between trains. While we were standing at the platform, chatting away to one another, I clocked another group of United lads coming through the station door. The mob was now between 90 and 100 strong.

We decided to pass the time at the station café, which turned out to be a massive error of judgement because one of the other customers randomly announced that the match was off. This gave all of the lads who didn't really want to go a weak excuse to bottle it.

'We're going to head back to Manc,' they said. 'We don't want to travel all the way down to The Smoke if there's nothing going down.'

The reality of the situation was that most of them hadn't wanted to travel down in the first place. They had been looking for a reason to call it a day and the supposed cancellation provided them with the perfect justification.

'Suit yourself,' I told them. 'I'm definitely going though.'

I was going to have a look about for Chelsea whether there was a game to see or not. We had a body count and there were 39 top boys, so we sang '39 Steps to Heaven' to the tune of 'Three Steps to Heaven' by Eddie Cochran while waiting for the train. We managed to make it all the way to London without the need for tickets. Now all we needed to do was jump the tube to Chelsea and walk to the ground.

'You're not going to make it back to your fackin' trains alive,' sneered a dreadlocked, mixed-race Chelsea lad as we made our way towards the stadium.

'Yeah right,' I told him. 'Just you wait and see.'

There was no segregation in those days and at least 3,000 unwanted red visitors turned up, which meant there was aggro from the minute we arrived at Stamford Bridge to the very end of the match. There was so much action on the terraces that I couldn't even begin to tell you what happened on the pitch. It was complete pandemonium for the entire 90 minutes.

Once the game had finished, we began to make our way back to Fulham Broadway station. We managed to make it onto the tube without anything going off, but then I ended up getting split up *from my friends and sitting further down the train, which left me feeling vulnerable. As I desperately scanned the seats for familiar faces, I spied a group of Chelsea lads walking through the carriage towards me. I was guaranteed to get a kicking if they realised I was a Red.*

'There's some Man U fans at the other end of the train,' one of these lads announced.

I nodded in acknowledgement, keeping my head down to avoid being recognised as an out-of-towner. I would have been in big trouble if he asked me anything that required a longer answer. My broad Mancunian accent would have given me away in seconds.

To my relief, the Chelsea supporters carried on down the carriage, assuming I was a Cockney. It was all a little too close for comfort. The atmosphere in the train was tense as fuck and I had a feeling it was about to go right off.

Sure enough, seconds later there was an almighty smashing sound and all of the windows on the train went through. Fifty to 60 tooled-up Chelsea lads had been waiting on the platform at Kensington High Street, ready to pelt us with bricks and iron rivets the moment we arrived. There was some work being done on the tracks, which provided them with a plentiful stock of missiles. The Chelsea dread had been spot on with his smartarse comments earlier; we were going to struggle to make it home in one piece.

Weekend shoppers desperately shielded their faces as shards of broken glass rained down. The doors on the train remained shut, preventing us from getting at the Cockneys. The only way we could reach them was by climbing through the broken windows, which seemed very risky because there were huge jagged edges everywhere.

Fuck it, I thought to myself. What have I got to lose?

As it turned out, I lost the feathers from my Kappa puffer jacket as I tore the lining open on a shard of glass. The entire carriage filled with a light white shower of down as the sharp, transparent spikes that protruded from our exit cut into the fabric. Chelsea were going to pay for this. It was time for me to do to them what they had done to my puffer.

Most of the rival lads armed themselves with makeshift tools, so I did likewise and picked up a hefty iron pole with a curve at the top. It looked a little bit like a shepherd's crook. The rest of our lads pulled off their huge, buckled Levi belts, ready to launch headfirst into the Cockneys. We were going to give our opponents a beating that they would never be able to forget. Both firms were now tooled up and looking to do some serious damage. This was going to be a battle and a half.

Chelsea stood their ground as 39 of United's gamest went steaming in. Sully punched a Cockney and knocked him under the train, forcing it to stay put for fear of running him over. We were causing untold levels of disruption, but that's the Red Devils for you: we left a trail of chaos behind us everywhere we went.

After ten long minutes of running battles, we finally managed to put our rivals on their toes. They attempted to retreat across the tracks but we weren't going to let them get away that easily. We chased them all the way along the line, trying our hardest to catch up with them to cement our victory. It was a miracle nobody got electrocuted by the third rail.

Unfortunately for us, PC Plod and his mates turned up before we were able to do our rivals any serious damage. They got there just in time to see a lad called Clint from Wythenshawe swinging one of those shepherd's crooks, which didn't go down too well. A couple of other boys got nicked for wielding scaffolding poles as well.

The Dibble forced us to walk all the way to Euston with them as an escort, which added two hours to our journey. They were so sick of United that they didn't care whether we had tickets home or not; they just shoved us on the first train back to Manny and told us to fuck off.

The minute we arrived at Piccadilly, we headed to a club called Kloisters on Oxford Road for a celebratory drink. The lads who had turned back at Stockport were in there, so we hurried over to fill them in on what had happened.

'You missed it! You missed a proper fucking mental battle,' I told them.

They had been deprived of one of the most exciting rows our crew has ever had. As we recounted our adventures, a look of disappointment formed on each one of the deserters' faces. It had been a fantastic day and any real football lad would love to have been there. The fact that I can still remember it so vividly today is testament to what a brilliant buzz it was.

Chelsea's boys were certainly no mugs. Soon after the train incident they became the notorious Headhunters, who have made the headlines time and time again. They had some handy lads onboard and put up a good fight, but no Cockney crew could have taken on United's legendary 39ers, not even in the capital. We stood our ground and fought with them when others would have melted. It's just a pity that I had to lose my top-of-the-range Kappa puffer jacket in the process.

Our battle that day was as fierce as fuck, but that's not to say that our rucks up north couldn't be just as naughty. It wasn't always the hooligans that took part in them either; sometimes the ordinary shirt-wearing fans would decide they wanted a pop and put up just as much of a fight. One of the craziest games I went to was a match against Newcastle in the 70s, when a load of Geordie barmies turned out to have a go. Back in those days there was no segregation, but the police had allocated us a section of the ground for this game because they knew a couple of hundred Reds were travelling up to Geordie Land. Around 800 Mancs turned up, including firms from Salford, Miles Platting, Wythenshawe and Stretford. Every area had its own little gang back then and they all teamed up to make a pretty hefty mob.

The police had decided that they were going to make all of our coaches park in an old cattle market, so we had to make our way from the market to the stadium without getting done in. The Geordies only had a mob of around 30 or 40 lads, but they were all twice our age and built like brick shithouses. They breed them tough in the North East: the Geordies wear only shirts in the winter and seem impervious to the cold. But some of their mob were pretty smartly dressed, wearing leather coats and wellies, something I'd never seen before.

I remember making a mental note of what the Newcastle lads had on, thinking, wow, that's different. Whenever we came across a firm that put their own twist on fashion, we would borrow elements from their look. We'd seen Brummies wearing shoes made of really hard material at a game against Birmingham and got some for ourselves, which proved a smart move because they were perfect for kicking the Geordies in their meat and two veg. When you're up against somebody twice your size, the only way that you can take them down is to belt them in the balls. One whack with those things was enough to leave our man-mountain opponents on the floor, holding their knackers for at least five minutes.

Woe betide any Geordie who ended up getting decked, as we would rob their wallets, rings, watches and sheepskins. Nobody had any money back in those days, so you needed to get your clobber how you could. A lot of lads came away with sheepskins a size too big for them, but this still beat not getting one at all. If you hesitated before taxing a jacket, somebody else would get in first. You needed to act fast. You didn't have time to size an item of clothing to see if it would fit; it was a case of hoping that you'd grow into whatever you could steal.

We eventually managed to fight our way into the ground and settled down to watch the game. It was a proper exciting match but we ended up getting beat 4-3, with Malcolm MacDonald scoring in the final ten minutes. The moment he put the goal in we knew the game was over, so we headed out of the ground. There was no point waiting until the Geordies mobbed up before making our move.

There were only a couple of Newcastle lads on the streets, so we quickly battered them and got off back to the cattle market. It was a good thing we left early, because an hour later the streets filled up with angry Newcastle shirters. They'd turned out to have a go at 500 United fans being escorted to their coaches. There must have been at least 150 coppers there but every one of them was needed as there was a sea of black and white, like a colony of penguins in the Arctic. I would say there were probably a good 4,000 Newcastle fans there, baying for Red Devil blood. If the Old Bill hadn't been there we would have had a right fight on our hands.

The word must have got round that we'd battered some Geordies before the game, because every single Newcastle supporter seemed intent on giving our fans a kicking. It was strange seeing so many shirters there who were up for it as it was usually only the hooligans who wanted a row. The image of 4,000 Geordie Magpies hurling abuse at our boys will stick in my mind until my dying day. It was an impressive sight, but wouldn't have been as pleasant if they had got their hands on us. It just goes to show that there's a hooligan inside every shirter waiting to get out.

Our run-in with the Geordies that day was heated to say the least, but wasn't a patch on our battles with our bitter blue neighbours. Warring with crowds of black-and-white barmies could never compare with going up against a team with whom we held a mutual enmity. There's nothing like having a row with a firm that you really, truly hate to get your adrenaline flowing. It was a step above your average fight at the football – with those cunts it was personal.

In the late 70s, we made a habit of going in the Kippax whenever we played The Shit away. We would go into the stadium in groups of two and three and join together inside to form a 50-strong mob. The first few punches that we threw were always guaranteed to get the City fans panicking. This would give the impression that there were more of us than there actually were, as it would be hard to tell who was City and who was United during the confusion. The bluenoses would sometimes end up running away from their own fans, which we all found hilarious.

We would also take it to the Blues' boozers. Rather than bowling up to them the minute we entered a pub, we would usually go to the back of the room and force them out of the front doors. Taking their pubs was similar to taking their end; it was a means of asserting our dominance over them. Invading bluenose boozers was our way of proving that we could go wherever we wanted.

When they were playing somewhere close like Leeds or Liverpool, we would wait for their football special to come back into Manchester and catch them unawares. Sometimes we would get them at the station, at other times we would lob bricks at their train partway through their journey. There was a spot in Miles Platting where you could climb over a fence and get right beside the tracks. City fans would always hang out of the windows with their scarves stretched out as they went past, which made them perfect targets for missiles. Looking back, it was a little bit out of order, but stoning trains is just one of those mad things you did when you were that age. We were on the receiving end of stonings when we went to away games so I know what it's like. It was especially common in Liverpool; the windows would go in as the train passed through Edgehill and we would all be forced to duck for cover.

I can only remember City taking us by surprise on the way back from a single away game. Two hundred of us had just come off the train at Oxford Road station, after beating Everton 2-0, when the word went round that the Blues were waiting for us near the Brunswick pub on London Road. As we approached the boozer we were greeted by their Kool Kats firm, armed with bottles and pint pots. The only reason they were willing to stand and have a go was because they were tooled up. They started backtracking the minute they'd used up all their ammunition, which was typical of City.

When a rival firm got on its toes, United never ran at them. We walked towards them at a steady pace because it was far more intimidating. This tactic soon had the Kool Kats scurrying away, which was to be expected because they usually weren't even brave enough to try and bushwhack us in the first place. Victory was ours, despite the attack being planned by the Blues rather than by ourselves. Overall, I would say we were the stronger of the two firms. City occasionally put up a bit of resistance but the Red Devils always stood our ground.

The Shit might not have been strong enough to take us but they were allied with a firm that could: the Greater Manchester Police. It's common knowledge that the majority of the Mancunian Old Bill are Blues, which means that City have less risk of being charged when they get arrested. You might think this is bollocks but I witnessed it firsthand at a derby game, when I got nicked with a couple of Blues.

The Old Bill must have been proper pissed off that day because United had just beaten City. The Blues started off winning 2-0 but we managed to pull it back to 2-2, and then Ryan Giggs scored in the final minute. Now it was just a case of leathering The Shit to celebrate.

As we walked past City's social club towards where the Indian restaurants are on Wilmslow Road, we saw a group of rival hooligans bowling down the street. They were fuming about the result and steamed straight into us. A raging battle ensued and United eventually got the upper hand. All of the City lads got off, so I started to make my way back home. Suddenly, a police officer came out of nowhere and told me to get down on the floor. The ground was soaking wet with rain so I refused point blank.

'Okay, you're under arrest then,' Officer Dibble told me.

He slapped the cuffs on me and shoved me in the back of a van. Four City lads and a United lad had also been arrested, the United lad accused of hitting a City fan with a chair leg.

'I know you're United fans but let me give you some advice,' the City lad told us as the Dibble drove us to the cop shop. 'When you get to the station, tell them you're Blues. If you're a Blue and it's your first time getting arrested, you'll get a caution.'

The test of whether he was telling the truth or not came when we got to Longsight police station.

'Who do you support then, lads?' the officer-in-charge asked us.

'City,' said the Blues, one after another.

'City,' lied the other Red.

I was just about to follow suit when another officer jumped in and cut me off. 'I know who you are, you red bastard,' he told me.

Uh-oh. This didn't bode too well.

With that the coppers ushered me into the station and locked me in an interview room. The cells were full of people who'd been arrested during the derby, so this was the only place that they had left to stick me. There was a hatch leading through to the reception area, presumably so the Dibble could pass papers through. This provided me with a perfect view of the charge desk. I could only stand and stare as the other lads from the van were handed their cautions.

I'm not having this, I thought. Like fuck they're all getting off and I'm getting a charge sheet!

My only chance of getting out was to make out I was injured. I scraped my shoe across the back of my neck until it bled, then pressed the buzzer on the door and waited for the Dibble to arrive.

'What do you want?' the officer who came to see me asked.

'I need to see a doctor,' I told him. 'I got hit on the neck by that City lad from Stretford that you arrested.'

The lad in question was actually the Red who had been pretending to be a Blue. I knew that he had already been released so I could lay the blame on him without him getting into trouble.

The Five-O seemed less concerned with my injuries and more interested in getting me locked up. I was eventually taken to the desk and charged, which proved beyond a shadow of a doubt that the police gave harsher punishments to Reds. The boys in blue are blue on the inside as well on the out.

Fortunately, the judge got straight onto the Old Bill's anti-United bias. Nineteen people were arrested that day: 18 City (including the Red who was posing as a Blue) and one United (me). The United fan was charged and the 18 City fans cautioned, despite the fact that one of the Blues had supposedly injured my neck. It was blatantly obvious that something was amiss. The case was eventually thrown out and I was allowed to go free.

The Dibble used every trick in the book to get us. If somebody was a known face on the scene then they'd have them whether they'd committed a crime or not. After a Spurs fan got killed at Seven Sisters tube station on the day of a United versus Tottenham game, I wasn't even at the station but still got accused of it. One officer really seemed to have it in for me. 'He's the killer,' he repeated over and over again, presumably hoping that he could get me off the streets for good.

Fortunately, the witnesses weren't as biased and didn't pick me out on the ID parade. The officer then went on to accuse somebody else, who also ended up walking free.

Two years later, I was travelling back from an away game at QPR on the same day Liverpool played Leicester. Me and my mate 'D' had successfully jibbed the train from Euston to Crewe, so all we needed to do was jump a train to Manchester and we would be home and dry. Unfortunately for us, a load of Scousers were waiting for the train from Crewe to Leicester; the place was swarming with Mickeys. We walked into a café to get a bite to eat and, the next thing I knew, we were surrounded by 200 bloodthirsty Liverpool lads. A few seasons prior to this, United had prevented Liverpool from winning the treble by beating them 2-1 at Wembley, with Jimmy Greenhoff and Lou Macari scoring our goals. The hatred that the Scousers harboured towards us was at an all-time high and they immediately kicked off.

The Mickeys bombarded us with cups, glasses and chairs as we desperately attempted to defend ourselves with plastic serving trays. They outnumbered us by a ratio of 100 to one, so the best that we could hope for was to stay alive. Partway through the scuffle, a load of Old Bill showed up, with an officer who looked just like the one that arrested me for the Seven Sisters incident heading the pack. The copper made his way through the hordes of rabid Scousers and slapped a pair of cuffs on me. Out of the 202 hooligans involved in the disturbance, I was the only one to be arrested.

I was taken to the police station, kept there until 11pm, charged and then released. The café was still open when I got back to the train station, so I decided to take some steps to clear my name while I was there.

'You saw what happened earlier, didn't you?' I asked the woman behind the counter. 'Is there any chance that you would be willing to make a statement saying that I was attacked and that I was defending myself?'

The lady told me that she would be happy to help and gave me her phone number. I wasn't in the wrong this time and didn't see why I should be punished for being jumped by a gang of Mickeys.

By the day of the court case, I'd managed to get an affidavit from the woman saying I'd acted in self-defence. My solicitor asked the copper if he'd ever arrested me before. The fella started stuttering and going red. I got a 'not guilty' verdict, which must have left him feeling gutted. The look on his face was priceless; I just wish I'd had a camera.

Back in the day, as far as the Old Bill were concerned, if you were black or of mixed race then you were automatically twice as guilty as anybody else involved in a brawl. I remember a semi-final game against Liverpool where the Dibble only arrested the black lads and ignored everybody else. Six black United fans were nicked despite the fact that the vast majority of people involved in the fight were white. The police always claimed to be upholding law and order, but in the 70s and 80s this only applied if you had the right colour skin.

The coppers also discriminated against people who they thought looked like hooligans. If you stood out because of your clobber or came across as a bit rough around the edges, you could be arrested for no reason at all. This happened at a game against Everton in the late 70s, when I got nicked for being chased by some Mickeys. I nearly ended up being charged too, even though the Dibble never saw me throw a punch.

United had a really big firm back then because a lot of top younger lads had worked their way up through the ranks. The trend for casual clothing had just hit, so a lot of the boys were kitted out in designer gear. Four hundred of us had been planning on invading Everton's main stand, but my mates and me had got there a little bit earlier than the rest and decided to go in on our own.

There were some coppers at the turnstiles looking out for Mancs, but we were well prepared for them. We had been practising Scouse accents on the train and managed to blag that we were locals. Whenever United played away, the boys would spend the journey pretending to be from various different places, in order to convince rival fans we were from the same city as them. This could make the difference between getting a kicking and being left alone. We could successfully imitate Cockneys, Brummies and Scousers, but Geordies were impossible. If you got surrounded by the home fans round that neck of the woods, you were pretty well fucked.

Once we'd got inside the stadium, we switched back to our natural accents and waited for the rest of the United lot to arrive. Unfortunately for us, the Scousers cottoned on to our presence before our reinforcements turned up and singled me out because I was mixed race. The next thing I knew, they were chasing me up and down the seats and I was running for my life.

The action eventually came to an end when a copper got a grip of me and told me I was being arrested for my own protection. I was surprised because I didn't know they could do that, but thought, I'm not arsed as long as they aren't charging me. The Dibble took me out of the ground, put me in a van and drove me to the police station. It was a bit of an inconvenience but at least I'd avoided being beaten to death by the Scousers.

After a stint in the cells, a copper took me out and told me I was being charged.

'Charged with what?' I asked him.

I couldn't believe the nerve of the fella. His colleague had already acknowledged I was the victim of a crime rather than the perpetrator; he was trying to stick me in the frame because of how I looked.

'You were fighting in the ground. Now what's your name and address?'

'I'm saying fuck all,' I told the cheeky twat. 'I was arrested for my own protection. I don't care if I stay here for months; you're not sticking it up me like this.'

I was eventually released. But in the 70s, if your face fitted the bill then the police were having you regardless of whether you'd thrown a punch or taken one.

Despite the Old Bill's dirty tricks, it was often me and the lads who had the final laugh. This was the case at an away game against West Brom, where we managed to get caught red-handed and still got set free. It was one of the most satisfying experiences of my life. We were coming out of the home end when the trouble that day first started. A couple of black and mixed-race Baggies tried to give us lip so we kicked off on them. The police soon arrived at the scene and arrested my mate and me, which was fair enough because we'd been brawling away like there was no tomorrow.

When the Old Bill put you in the back of their van, they usually ask your name and assign you a number. On this particular occasion they'd forgotten to do this, which meant that when we got to the police station there was no record of who had done what.

'Whose are these two Mancs?' the police sergeant asked the coppers from the van.

The number assigned to you when you're nicked shows which cop has taken you in. Without it, there was no record of our arrests being authorised.

'They're not mine,' said the copper who had driven the van.

'Well they're not mine either,' said his fellow OB.

'It's your lucky day then,' the sergeant told us. 'They don't know who arrested you so you're going to be de-arrested and set free.'

The officers from the van looked absolutely gutted. They knew that we were getting off on a minor technicality and it was eating them up.

The fact that we were laughing probably didn't help either. We were over the moon that we were being released and couldn't have hidden it if we'd tried.

'Get back in the van,' shouted an incredibly pissed-off-looking copper.

We did as he commanded and six of his colleagues piled into the back with us. The driver took us into the middle of the countryside whilst the other boys in blue beat seven shades of shit out of us. It still beat getting a charge sheet any day of the week.

It took us over an hour to find our way back to West Brom from where the police had abandoned us. We didn't have a clue where we were and had to ask the locals for directions. When we arrived back at the station, we'd missed the last direct train home and had to travel back via Birmingham. It was a pain in the arse but it was worth it for the look on the Old Bill's faces alone. It was a case of United 1, Coppers 0. Our narrow escape was payback for all the times the police have tried to stitch people up because of their race or how they dressed.

Nowadays the Old Bill are not half as bad as they used to be. They have tried it on so many times and had their fingers burnt that they're a lot warier. The cops of today are probably just as biased and horrible as they were back then, but there are better systems in place for keeping them in line and for reporting police brutality.

The fact that Coco was willing to take the coppers on shows how fearless he was, because the Old Bill didn't fuck about. If the boys in blue were gunning for you then, you definitely knew about it. The respect and admiration he received from within the firm spurred me on to further my own reputation. Throughout the mid-80s, I forged a reputation for myself amongst the younger lads and older lads alike, throwing myself into every battle that we had and soon becoming one of United's main faces. Now it would be just a case of building on my success.

10
Nottingham Forest

The late 80s was the period when the name 'Hotshot' first gained proper clout. Terraces up and down the country buzzed with talk of a pint-sized hooligan and his fresh-faced firm of game-as-fuck young thugs. Up-and-comers started admiring us as well, just as we'd looked up to the General and his mates when we first came on the scene. I'd progressed from a lad who was respected by those in the know to one of the top boys in the crew.

The Gallaghers gained just as much of a rep for themselves. They stood out because they were twins, which brought a lot of unwanted attention from rival mobs their way, but yet they never let the fact that other firms were gunning for them put them off a row. The three of us had always covered each other's backs, no matter who we were up against, and refused to walk away from a fight.

We weren't the only lads to rise up through the ranks either; a group of younger Cockney Reds had also started making a name for themselves. We first became aware of this eager firm at a game against Coventry in '87, when we saw them walking down the street and almost had it with them because we thought they were a rival mob. After being assured that they supported the same team as us, we struck up a conversation and realised they were all sound lads. Boys like Fry, Bigzy, Walker and Carter soon became big names in our firm.

As well as new allies, we also gained new enemies. Up until this point our main opponents had always been City and Liverpool but an unpleasant encounter with Notts Forest placed their Forest Executive Crew up there alongside The Shit and the Scousers. The Notts lads took their name from their Executive Stand and had their battles with bitter rivals Derby compared in court to a 'Northern Ireland battlefield'. Their mob contained a lot of ex-coalminers and most of them had the physique of Giant Haystacks, which meant they were difficult to take down. You know the saying though: 'The bigger they are, the harder they fall.'

Our rivalry with the FEC started at an FA Cup game at Old Trafford in the late 80s. The Forest fans sang Munich songs for the full 90 minutes, which pissed off everybody in our stands, not only our hooligans. The action on the pitch was equally infuriating, as Bryan Robson bundled the ball in off the back post at the very last minute only for the referee to say it hadn't crossed the line. This caused us to lose 1-0 and wound everybody up to fever pitch. By the time the final whistle went, we were fucking furious. The Forest lads were going to feel our wrath; they were, as the chant goes, going to get their fucking heads kicked in.

The Old Bill let both sets of supporters out of the stadium at the same time, which they never usually do. This was a major error of judgement because the rival fans were still singing their Munich songs. The entire forecourt erupted into violence as a sea of United went flying into them. The majority of the people throwing punches weren't even our thugs; they were just your average, run-of-the-mill supporters who had had enough. There were even old men in team colours getting involved, which shows the level of hatred the Forest fans had evoked. There is only so much abuse a team can take. Our rivals had clearly overstepped the mark and it was time for them to be punished.

There were so many people involved in the row that it was impossible to work out who was who. The barmies were punching anybody and everybody in the hope of injuring a rival fan. The Old Bill seemed reluctant to get involved, which was bizarre given the scale of the disturbance. Maybe they'd heard what the Forest fans had been singing and decided to let us give it to them. Whatever the reason for their unwillingness to intervene, the violence went on for a full 20 minutes, which is a ridiculously long time for a mass brawl like that. One of the Cockney Reds decided to head for home partway through the fight because he had a train to catch. He walked up to the top of Warwick Road, where the chippies are, then changed his mind and launched himself back into the fray. It was too good an opportunity to pass up – it isn't every day that the streets become a giant free-for-all.

By the time the Old Bill finally got the situation under control, one of the Forest lads had been stabbed and countless other people were nursing injuries. The FEC had stood and fought for the entire 20 minutes, which marked them out as a firm to watch. We were looking forward to the next time they crossed our paths so that we could have another pop. They were now filed away, alongside Man City and the Scousers, as a mob we would have it with whenever our team played theirs.

We didn't have to wait too long to see the Forest lot again, as we bumped into a big group of their boys at an England versus Scotland game six months down the line. They'd firmed up with a mob of West Ham and wanted to know if we'd join their ranks.

'Fuck off!' was our answer. 'We don't go with nobody. We're on our own and we don't want no cunts with us!' They were cheeky fuckers for thinking we would team up with them after all the abuse they'd given us at Old Trafford.

'They think they're fucking it,' complained one of the Forest lads. 'We could have had the perfect firm to do the Jocks.'

There was a murmur of agreement from the FEC and, the next thing I knew, a group of 20 of them had come right up close to us and started giving us shit. We went straight into the whining bastards, slapping them about the place until they backed away. We would have fucking leathered them if one of our lads hadn't intervened and told us to leave it out.

'They're not worth it. They're a load of fucking mugs, the lot of them.'

He had a point as well; they'd made it obvious that they weren't up for a row by getting on their toes the minute we fronted up. United don't take liberties. We will only ever take on firms that are looking for it, which meant that we would have to wait until the next time we played their team to wipe the floor with them.

The fact that we had refused to join the Forest/West Ham alliance made the FEC hate us even more. They saw our unwillingness to team up as a sign that we were arrogant, but the reality of the situation was that United have never been a mob to firm up at internationals. Mancs are similar to Scousers in that we identify ourselves by our city rather than our nationality. We are Mancunian first and English second, so why would we ever align ourselves with another team just because we're both from England? It was United or nothing as far as we were concerned. Notts Forest could fuck off.

By the time we played their team again, the FEC had got it into their heads that we needed taking down a peg. We had rudely spurned their offer to join forces, which got their knickers in a twist.

We were drinking at a pub just outside Nottingham train station, before a Sunday night game, when two of Forest's black lads came bowling through the door to challenge us to a row, shouting, 'Come on, boys, we're here.' They were giving it the big 'un, trying to act as if their mob was something to be scared of. Martin and me gave them a couple of slaps and the rest of the firm chucked pint pots at them as they scurried out of the pub.

'Go and get your fucking firm then,' I shouted. 'Fucking bring it on, you wankers! You know where we are.'

I raced out of the boozer, ready to give the Notts lads some more shit, and saw another 50 of their boys hiding behind a row of Dibble. They were trying their hardest to look as though they were up for it; but it was clear to all and sundry that they were using the Old Bill for protection. They wanted to show their faces but didn't want to get done in. What a fucking joke.

Realising that we were unlikely to get a row, we decided to make our way towards the ground. We saw a couple of FEC along the way but none of them showed any signs of bringing it on. What had happened to the Forest boys wanting to teach us a lesson for refusing to firm up? We were marching around their manor without any opposition.

Just as we were beginning to think that Forest had forgotten all about their little grudge, we noticed a couple of their lads milling around outside a boozer on a rundown housing estate. Bingo! We'd stumbled across their watering hole.

There was a partly demolished wall nearby, so we quickly armed ourselves with bricks and pelted Forest's pub until five of their boys came running to the entrance. One of our lads ripped off part of the door and whacked some poor cunt over the head with it. The lads at the front of the FEC were in a bit of a predicament, trapped in the line of fire by the crowd that had gathered to their rear. They ended up getting absolutely hammered.

The police took a good three minutes to arrive, which is quite a long while for a raid on a pub to continue. None of us fancied getting nicked and missing out on the match, so we headed off to the ground shortly after they turned up. It was looking to be quite an exciting game because the word went round that Alex Fergusson would lose his job if United didn't win. We had our fingers firmly crossed that it wouldn't come to that.

Fortunately for Fergie we ended up beating Forest 1-0, with Mark Robins scoring our goal. We were buzzing about our victory and couldn't wait to leather the FEC to celebrate. The minute we were allowed out of the ground, 25 of our younger lads slipped away from the Old Bill and went off looking for Forest's mob. It was a horrible, dark, wet, rainy night, but we were unwilling to let the shitty weather deter us from our mission. It was going to take much more than a spot of drizzle to break our spirit; we had set out to give those Forest cunts a kicking and that was exactly what we were going to do.

After what seemed like an eternity of traipsing around Nottingham city centre in the rain, a couple of the lads suggested calling it a day. 'It's fucking pissing it down and the whole city is deserted,' said J. 'We obviously aren't going to find them so let's fuck off back home.'

We were walking towards the station with the intention of jumping on the next train back to Manchester when we spotted about 70 shady-looking figures spreading out across the road. Usually, rival lads will be singing and shouting after a game, but this lot were as quiet as a mouse. It was as if they had been laying silently in wait.

'Stand your ground,' one of the boys announced as our opponents advanced along the street. They were a fair bit older than our mob but that was the norm whenever we faced a rival firm. It had gotten to the stage where it was impossible to take lads of our own age seriously. On the few occasions when we got to fight with other teenage mobs, I'd be so used to having it with fully grown men that I'd spend the whole time thinking, *Come back in a couple of years' time, then maybe we'll get a decent row.* It wasn't that I was arrogant, I was just used to fighting blokes with beards and beer bellies.

Martin didn't give a fuck how old the FEC lads were; all he cared about was handing them their arses on a plate. The minute they came within range he was upon them, showing no fear whatsoever. The rest of our boys were straight in after him. We were badly outnumbered but that wasn't going to prevent us from giving it our all. We were determined to send the FEC home covered in their own blood.

The fight went on for a good five minutes before the Old Bill showed up. I wouldn't say that either firm came out on top, but we had a lot less lads than Forest did so it was more of a result for us. We had done well for ourselves, considering the fact that our mob was around a third of the size of theirs. As we were escorted to the station by the police, I felt a wave of satisfaction washing over my body. It was yet another job well done.

Whenever we played a team in the East Midlands, we would always go on to Chesterfield after the post-match violence. It's the perfect place to celebrate a battle because it's full of top-notch fanny. We spent the remainder of the night getting pissed and Charlied up. The United boys had stood their ground against a mob of fully-grown men. We were buzzing about the row for weeks to come and chalked it up as another major success.

We were lucky to get a good, clean fight against the FEC because they are another firm that have victimised lone United lads in the past. This is something that a certain master pickpocket has firsthand experience of, being on the receiving end of a cowardly attack by a big mob of Notts Forest after a game at Old Trafford – although the incident in question left one of their boys wishing he'd stayed at home. Here's what BV has to say about his run-in with a firm of liberty-taking wankers who bit off more than they could chew:

BV

I was on my way to do some dipping when I first saw Forest's lads. The match was about to finish and I was looking forward to relieving the fans of their cash. I didn't expect for a single minute that the FEC would target somebody who was on their own. They were all six-foot ex-miners, so what would they have to prove by doing something like that?

As it turned out, the Forest boys were a bunch of dishonourable shitbags who didn't give a fuck how badly outnumbered I was. One of their lads gave me a crack completely out of the blue and sent me flying onto the floor. I landed face first on the concrete and chipped my bottom teeth.

'That fucking bastard's smashed my Newton Heaths!' I shouted.

I was the spit of Justin Timberlake back then. I had a stylish flick haircut and prided myself on my appearance. Those dirty Forest twats had fucked up my good looks. It was time for them to pay.

By this stage, the rest of our firm had arrived on the scene. One of our boys was walking down the pavement towards me so I pointed my assailant out to him.

'Get him!' I yelled, my entire body bristling with rage. 'That cunt needs sorting out!'

I don't know if any of the United lot managed to catch up with the fella who put me on the floor but somebody definitely got it, because there was an article in the paper the following day saying that a Forest supporter lost an eye. There was a rumour going round that the victim was stabbed by one of our boys.

Nottingham Forest

Despite the odd incident where they picked off smaller groups of lads, Forest are easily up there with the best of them. They may have taken advantage of BV but they can definitely hold their own against a firm of equal numbers. I'd rank them as the top East Midlands mob, although their bitter rivals, Derby County, also had a firm to be reckoned with. Their Derby Lunatic Fringe crew provided us with some stiff competition; they might not have quite been up to the FEC's standard but they were still as game as fuck.

11
Derby Lunatic Fringe

The Derby lads were similar to their rivals in that they were all hulking great bodybuilder types. They seem to breed them big in the East Mids. There were a couple of times when we had to use weapons against them; although we were easily able to take on any firm we came up against, there was always the odd occasion when we needed to take things up a notch. One away game in the late 80s springs to mind: between 15 and 20 of ours lads were walking to Derby's ground when a group of 20-odd DLF came bowling down the street. We didn't even realise who they were at first; as far as we were concerned they were just a random group of lads.

As the DLF drew level with us, one of them cracked Martin in the face and the street descended into chaos. A United lad from Droylsden got knocked clean out with a single punch. The Derby lot were all a good few years older than our mob and some of them were built like brick shithouses. They had a lot of lads who looked as if they had been fed on creatine from birth.

One of our boys was getting stuck into a Derby kid when another DLF member came over to try and pull him off. This was a bad move on the part of the fella that intervened because our lad went to work on him, leaving him bleeding from the bottom of his ear to the middle of his neck. The Derby lad didn't even seem to realise he was dripping with claret. It's only when you see blood that you start panicking after something like that has taken place.

Partway through the row, a white van pulled up at the side

of the road and seven more Derby lads piled out onto the street. We usually wouldn't be the least bit fazed by our rivals having a couple more boys than us but, for whatever reason, I found myself running for my life. The rest of our mob did exactly the same, which was a bit embarrassing.

'We're United, we can't get done like this,' one of the lads complained as we stopped to catch our breath around the corner from where the fight had kicked off. 'Let's go back and do the cunts.'

We were the unbeatable Red Devils; we couldn't allow ourselves to be done by a mob of out-of-work coal miners.

The rest of the lads armed themselves with bricks while I picked up a broken exhaust box off the floor. Now that we were all tooled up, it was time for us to turn the situation around. The DLF were still chasing after us, which meant we didn't even have to move. The minute they caught up with us we flew into the bastards, eager to make up for our show of legs. This time it was Derby's turn to run. They were on their toes as soon as they realised we were going to stand our ground.

'Fucking hell!' said C. 'At least we've got a bit of a result here now.'

We were still perplexed by our initial retreat. The Red Army doesn't run; it was very uncharacteristic of our firm.

The DLF had proven themselves a worthy opponent. They may have eventually lost the battle but they got us on our toes, which is no small feat. They were no joke and I have to admit I was left with a grudging sense of respect for them. Fair play to their lads: they put up a valiant effort and did what many firms had failed to do, in momentarily breaking the resolve of one of the country's gamest sets of lads.

There were no further kickoffs that day, which was disappointing because we would have liked another victory over the Derby boys. But we'd had a row and managed to turn a losing battle around, which was good enough for me. There have been plenty of other times when the DLF came a cropper at the hands of United. Makeshift weapons found on the ground were not the only tools used either. BV tells me he once saw a Red Army lad called Harry the Blade reaching his hand towards one of their faces and thought Harry was taking the fella's glasses off him. As he drew a bit closer, he realised he'd been cutting the lad across the mug.

'I'm not a fan of people using blades but still thought Derby asked for it,' says BV. 'Three hundred of them would have no qualms whatsoever about steaming into ten of us. What goes around comes around and besides, if you're a football lad then getting stabbed or slashed is just a risk you have to take.'

Blades divide opinions. Some think they are necessary to teach rivals a lesson when they've taken liberties; others think they should never be used, no matter what the circumstances. I can't say I'm the biggest fan of going to games tooled up, but at the end of the day there will always be people who do it – whether it's frowned upon or not. Derby have done the dirty on us in the past, so they can hardly complain. If you go to a match looking for trouble there's always a chance that you'll get cut. The victim knew the score before he left home for a scrap.

Slashing people up was a last resort for United. It only happened every now and then as we were more than capable of fighting with our fists. Unfortunately, some of the other mobs were a little bit fonder of using Stanleys. The Scousers were the worst, as I've already said; their older lads were bad enough, but in 1987 we came across a younger crew of Mickeys even more intent on hacking us to pieces than their predecessors. They were one of the few youth firms that we saw as a threat: Liverpool's Urchins crew, the mob that made it their mission to slash both me and the Gallaghers.

12
Urchin Sam

I was around 16 when I first came across the Urchins and hated them from the moment I laid eyes on them. There was nothing personal in it; Mancs just don't like Scousers. We were at Euston station in London at the time and I remember thinking, *Who do these cunts think they are?* We didn't come to blows with them because neither of us had numbers with us, but I made a mental note to have a piece of them when they next crossed our paths. One lad in particular really stuck in my mind because he was black and the Mickeys didn't have many minorities onboard. I remember thinking he must have some balls to knock about with a firm so notorious for racism. The only other black Scouse hooligan I'd heard of was an Everton lad called Joe and the rest of their mob had nicknamed him 'Joe the Coon', which says it all really.

We kept seeing this young black Mickey whenever we came up against the Urchins and I soon realised he was one of their main players. He was small like me, but game as fuck, and always seemed to be in the thick of it. His name was Sam and he was definitely a front-liner. The rest of the Scousers seemed to respect him and had good reason to, as he was proper up for it.

A Cockney Liverpool supporter called Leroy who is a good friend of mine, got to know this Scouse scallywag quite closely. Whenever Liverpool played at home, Mo would stay at his North African aunt and uncle's house in Toxteth, which was near the area where Sam lived. It's only fair to let him give a Liverpool perspective, given that I've already included a chapter from our other rivals, the Young Guvnors:

HOTSHOT

LEROY

Liverpool is a very white city. People tend to stereotype the Liverpool 8 postcode as a black area, but the reality is that there's only a small part of Toxteth with anybody black living there. Sam grew up in Dingle, which is on the white side of L8. The whole of Liverpool was very gang-orientated back then, but L8 was especially territorial. The local school was the site of constant wars between the whites and blacks. This was weird for Sam because most of his friends were white. Nobody even saw him as black though; they just saw him as one of the Dingle boys.

At age 12, Sam caught his first glimpse of football violence. He was standing in the Kop before kickoff when it went off proper in the Anfield Road End. The rush of adrenaline he got from witnessing something so dangerous gave him shivers down his spine. It was definitely an activity he wanted to get involved in when he was older.

Three years later, Sam went to a game against Man City with his older brother, 'H'. It was a cold, dark winter's night and the Liverpool supporters were set upon by a crew of City after the match. H stood with some of the older Scouse lads and fought back against the Mancs, which gained him the respect of his peers. The other Liverpool boys didn't even think about this gutsy black kid's race; they just saw him as somebody unwilling to back down.

Sam's brother soon became a well-known face at Anfield. He would never run away, no matter how big his opponent. If he came up against a rival who was twice his size then he'd use a blade. That was H's way of evening up the score; the lad was never shy of giving someone's mug a stripe. People like to tarnish Scousers with the label 'slashers', but most of the firm would only ever carry knives for protection. The minute someone pulled a chiv out, a rival mob would back away. If it came down to it, our lads would give a geezer's face a little cut but never aimed to kill or injure anybody. It was just a means of letting an opponent know these boys meant business.

The chivs of choice were little red craft knives because they were easier to conceal. The lads would cut a secret compartment into their jeans to hide them. To my knowledge, none of the main Scouse firm ever got caught with one of these blades in all the time I went to games. They were a lot subtler than the old carpet carvers that were used in Liverpool in the 70s; those things could slice somebody's nose and lips apart in an instant. Craft knives could be used to deliver a swift little cut to the cheek without fear of permanently disfiguring someone.

Blades got H and his pals out of a couple of tight spots. I remember when he was surrounded by a mob of Middlesbrough and had to slash a lad across the face to get away. The Boro boys were built like shithouses and had a major rivalry with Liverpool. If he hadn't had his blade on him, H would have got the kicking of his life. Another time he was getting his arm chewed up by a police dog and someone had to take a Stanley to its arse to get it off. The poor thing was yelping like crazy.

The first time Sam became involved in the action himself was at a midweek away game against Arsenal. He'd lied to his schoolteacher and told her he had a dentist's appointment so that he could see his team. Him and his mates jibbed their way into the home end and had it with the London boys. A Scouse lad got slashed across the hands and the Liverpool lot ended up running out onto the pitch. Sam had the time of his life and couldn't wait until the next time it kicked off.

As it happened, he didn't need to wait too long because the Scousers were ambushed by a couple of hundred Arsenal fans on their way back to the station. One of Sam's mates got caught trying to run away and was promptly smashed to fuck. The rest of the lads managed to make it to their train in one piece and vowed to stick with the main mob at the next game. They'd learnt how naughty it could get while seeing their team away and how they needed to travel to and from the ground in numbers to avoid being picked off.

Over the years, Sam got to know Liverpool supporters from all over the city. His friends soon developed their own little crew, which consisted of lads from Speke, Garston, Dingle, Norris Green, Croxteth, Netherley, Kirkdale, Anfield, Everton, Scotland Road and Knowsley. There were a couple of boys from London and Carlisle thrown into the mix as well, but most of the firm were Scousers.

A lot of people like to portray Liverpool's mob as racist, but I'd say that some lads were just ignorant. They would use words like 'nigger' quite a lot to wind up the minorities, but never once gave Sam any stick for being black. I'd go as far as to say I've never met a football lad who was a hardcore racist. Some were politically incorrect and referred to minorities using racial slurs, but that was the full extent of their prejudice.

Nowadays, Sam's firm are known as the Urchins, but back when they started they made a conscious decision not to have a name. The minute they gave themselves an official title they knew they'd get unwanted attention from the Old Bill, so they were simply known as the 'younger Liverpool lads'.

Sam soon found that being a hooligan meant he had an army available to fight his corner whenever he needed it. If anybody ever picked on his younger sister, or gave his parents cheek, he could assemble a mob of 50 to 100 lads within the hour. Dingle wasn't a massive area for hooliganism, but there were enough Urchins in the surrounding areas for him to get a firm together at a moment's notice. His family were glad of the security that came with being part of a mob, although they didn't know the full extent of what went on at the football. They just assumed the crew travelled to the games together for safety in numbers, in case anything kicked off.

As well as providing protection on the tough streets of South Liverpool, being a hooligan also had financial benefits as there was a big culture of grafting amongst our lads. That's what set Liverpool apart from Everton: most of the Blues had fulltime jobs but the majority of the Urchins were professional criminals. There was a similar division in London: Chelsea were upstanding members of society compared to the likes of Millwall and West Ham. The Bushwhackers and the ICF

Urchin Sam

were typical Cockney wide-boy types who made their money in the same way as the Urchins.

Sam and his mates were like characters from Oliver Twist. Some of them were dippers, some were shoplifters and others made their cash through smash and grabs. Sometimes they would travel to Switzerland en masse to pillage all the well-to-do French towns. They were very much like the Mancs in this respect; the phenomenon of criminally minded football firms was definitely a north-western thing.

A lifestyle consisting entirely of fighting and grafting has its inevitable pitfalls and Sam had his fair share of brushes with the law. One time he was on his way to a Portsmouth game when he got pulled by the Old Bill. They took him down to the station but failed to find a thing, despite the fact he had a blade down one side of his shoe and some weed down the other. This is either testament to how good Scousers are at hiding things or proof that most coppers are thick.

The other main pitfall to hooliganism was being badly outnumbered and getting kicked to fuck, which almost happened to the Urchins on the day they first met Hotshot and the Gallaghers. Liverpool and Man U were playing away in London and the Scousers had planned to ambush the United boys at Crewe station. Both firms were scheduled to change trains there and it would have been the perfect place to bushwhack the Red Army if Liverpool hadn't only 50 boys onboard. Fortunately for them, they were unable to find the Mancs, which saved them from a kicking. Respect to them for turning out with only a handful of hooligans, but they'd have been completely swamped by Red Devils.

The Urchins bumped into Hotshot and a couple of his mates at Euston station later on that day and had a chinwag with them. Shot told Sam he had seen the Scousers on the platform at Crewe but remained where he was because there were only a couple of Red Army lads on the train he'd travelled down on. Fuck knows where the rest of United's mob were; they must have arrived before or after our lot.

Sam and his mates said their goodbyes to Hotshot and headed off

127

to get some food. They were queuing up in a chippy when there was a sudden shout of 'United!' and a huge mob of Man U came charging down the road towards them. The Urchins were taken by surprise and bolted up a nearby hill. As they reached the summit, one of the older lads looked back and said, 'Fuck that, there's only a few of them!' This was the only encouragement the other Scousers needed. Within a split second they'd tooled themselves up with bricks and bottles from a nearby skip and turned around to face the manky Mancs. Sam belted the nearest Man U lad in the head with a wine bottle, sending him staggering backwards. The rest of the Liverpool lads followed suit and, before they knew it, they'd evened up the score and held their own against the firm they initially ran from.

The meeting with Hotshot stuck in our lads' minds because the little fella had an unusual nickname and a very distinctive appearance. He was half the size of the other Red Devils and looked half their age as well. Although he wasn't present for the battle on the hill, a lot of our boys still vowed they were going to slash him up. Every time we played Man U, our younger hooligans would be saying, 'We'll catch him today. That little fucker's getting cut.'

Year after year, the Urchins swore Hotshot was getting a stripe at the next game. I think the main thing that prevented him getting a Stanley across his face was that Liverpool didn't actually have that many battles with Man U. There were always a lot of cops around because it was such a big game, which prevented very much going off.

Liverpool had more run-ins with Man City than they did with United. City's ground was full of dodgy little backstreets, which provided a lot more scope for ambushes. A couple of our lot nearly got done by the Guvnors at the foodcourt in London Euston. They were getting a bite to eat before a Liverpool v. Chelsea game when a 200-strong mob of Mancs came bowling through the door, grinning from ear to ear. One of them put a Stanley to Sam's knee and asked Benny, who was City's leader at the time, for permission to cut him.

'Leave it out,' said Benny. 'There's only a few of them.'

Urchin Sam

He was a decent lad and didn't believe in taking liberties. The Mancs and Scousers ended up going to City's game at West Ham together and having it with the Cockneys. There was a ruck outside the ground before kickoff and a couple of incidents afterwards. Taking on the Hammers must have been a lot more satisfying for the City boys than slashing a handful of our lads would have been. Kudos to them for picking firm-on-firm action over an easy but dishonourable result.

The rivalry between the Scousers and the Mancs is a weird one, because when they meet abroad, in criminal hotspots like Amsterdam and the Costa Del Sol, they always get on well. I think Liverpudlians and Mancunians definitely have more in common than the residents of either city do with Londoners. They have a similar culture and the same grafting mentality. The enmity probably stems from the fact that Manchester has more money spent on it than Liverpool: the Mancs have got a bigger airport, fancy tram system and better shops. All Liverpool has got is its top-notch football team and game lads like the Urchins. Mind you, when it comes to the football, that's all it ever really needs.

13
Scarlet Ribbon

The late 80s might have been the period when we gained a new set of enemies in the form of Sam and his mates, but it was also the time we picked up the first ever female member of our mob. The one thing more dangerous than being a lad and going to matches with the likes of the Urchins on the prowl is being a bird and doing likewise. This was the case for Scarlet Ribbon, the only girl to be accepted into the fold.

I first met Scarlet in the Merchants pub on Oldham Street in Manchester city centre, one of United's main boozers. She seemed to know all of the local faces, whether City or United, and gave the impression that she was comfy around thugs. We soon got talking and I was impressed by what a dedicated United fan she was. It's rare to find a girl who is truly passionate about football but she really knew her stuff.

The following match day, I was surprised to see Scarlet heading off to the game with our lads.

'What the fuck's she doing here?' I asked Martin. 'She might get herself hurt.'

I'd never known a bird to go to a game with the boys before. Although a lot of football lads would have reservations about hitting a girl, there was still a high chance of her getting caught up in something.

It took a while for me to get my head around Scarlet. She wasn't like other girls. She was really into her football and didn't seem to mind being around people who attracted trouble. As she went to more and more matches with us, I gradually began to accept her as one of the lads. The real turning point came when she saved Galley from getting done by a load of Young Guvnors. They were jumping all over his head, so she flung herself over him and shielded his body with hers. If it wasn't for her, he probably would have ended up in hospital.

For that alone she deserves a mention in this book. But I've also given her a chapter of her own to explain what it's like to be a girl in the male-dominated arena of the hooligan:

SCARLET

I will never forget the first time I went down to Old Trafford in the mid 70s, with my dad and eldest brother. I felt a tremendous rush as I walked down Warwick Road, holding tightly onto my dad's hand. The buzz amidst the sea of red, white and black was electrifying; the chanting of the fans and the smell of fish and chips were overwhelming. I can't recall who we were playing and, if I'm honest, I don't think I watched much of the game because I was far too captivated by the aura of Old Trafford. I was more interested in gazing around in amazement at the full house. The atmosphere was intense and you could feel the passion and adoration in the air. I immediately knew I'd stumbled across something special.

Being brought up on an estate that was predominantly male, and having two older brothers, meant I was always knocking about with lads and became something of a tomboy. Growing up it was always cricket in the summer and football in the winter. I didn't actually get involved myself because the lads who played were all a lot older, but I still loved watching them. I enjoyed the banter and the laughs. Sometimes, if I was lucky (or maybe, on reflection, unlucky), somebody would ask me to go in net for Wembley doubles, headers and volleys, or 60 seconds. I would spend the afternoon getting the ball booted at me full blast and usually ended up ducking and diving to avoid a stinger. This probably stood me in good stead for later life.

Scarlet Ribbon

Another memory from the 70s is Merlin's football stickers, which I must have spent a packet on. I took my sticker book and my swaps everywhere with me, studying the players at every available moment. I never did manage to complete the album but got about 20 John Hibberts.

Being from a working-class family, we didn't go to the match on a regular basis and it was always a bit of a treat when we did. I still made sure I'd follow all the games though: I would listen to the live commentary on a transistor radio because football was rarely shown on TV at the time.

The FA Cup Final was an eagerly anticipated event in our household, regardless of who was playing. I will always remember the semi-final replay against Liverpool in 1979, which was a mid-week fixture. I was only nine and wasn't allowed to stay up to listen to it on the radio because I had school in the morning. There was no way I was going to miss it though: Liverpool were our biggest rivals, so we had to do the business. I snuck my little transistor under the blanket in my bed and lay there listening to the commentator, hanging onto every word while trying to keep an ear open for my mum or dad coming upstairs.

Partway through the second half, the commentator started talking about Lou Macari struggling with his fitness and signalling to come off-pitch.

No, *I thought to myself,* we don't need this!

Suddenly the commentator said, 'McIlroy is just inside ... Greenhoff's far post ... JIMMY GREENHOFF! Manchester United have scored! And it's the man who scored in last year's final ... JIMMY GREENHOFF! The master craftsman was in the right place at the right time!'

I loved Jimmy Greenhoff and was over the moon that he had scored. Unable to contain my happiness, I jumped out of my bed and started screaming and crying tears of joy. My mum and dad came running up the stairs and burst into my bedroom to find me doing a rain dance.

HOTSHOT

'What's wrong? What's happened?' asked my dad.

'It's Jimmy Greenhoff,' I shouted, 'he's scored!'

The looks on their faces were priceless.

I was still knocking about with older lads when I was in secondary school and asked my dad if I could go with friends to Old Trafford one weekend, around 1984. At the time I'd been going to the games sporadically with my dad, but it wasn't regular and I wanted to start going with my mates. He wasn't having it though, so I just went anyway.

I was really buzzing about going to my first match without my old man. We were playing Tottenham Hotspur, and it was my first experience of United Road. I'd always been used to the safety of the seats in the K Stand when I went with my dad, and relished the thought of getting on the terraces. When I saw what they were like, I could appreciate why he was apprehensive about me going to matches on my own. It was very lairy in there. We were crammed in like sardines and the noise was deafening, with the Red Army singing non-stop.

We were in the corner and the away fans were in the paddock next to us. When United scored, a load of coins came raining down and some poor lad in front of me got hit with a ten-bob bit on the bone just above his eye. The skin covering the bone split open as the coin made contact. There was also some mental guy who must have been well over six foot and was dressed in a full-length Nazi-style trench-coat. He gave the away fans abuse about the Jews for the full 90 minutes, which made me wonder what the fuck he was going on about. I wasn't aware that Tottenham's board was mainly made up of Jews at the time.

Another thing that surprised me was that, when they needed to go, everyone pissed where they were stood. As well as dodging missiles flying over, I was also dodging the rivers of piss that flowed down the terraces.

I'd told my dad that I was going into town but arrived home at around seven, which was suspicious because most places in town shut at five. My dad demanded an explanation, so I came up with some old rubbish about getting lost and being unable to find the bus stop. He asked me if I'd been to Old Trafford and I admitted it, but managed to persuade him to let me go with my mates in future. This was a result.

So that was the beginning of my match days — and what days they were! I used to go to the games with the lads from school and go in a pub off Deansgate called the Vic when the match had finished. I think being the only girl made me stand out a little bit. I was never really a shrinking violet and could talk a glass eye to sleep, so I gradually got to know people from all over Manchester. The lads from school didn't go to all the matches, so I eventually started going into town on my own. I knew that I'd always bump into someone I knew. I'd just get off the bus in the city centre and go into a pub where it was a dead cert that there would be fellow United supporters.

I loved going in the Merchants on Oldham Street before the game. Brannigan's was another favourite haunt during the 80s. Even when the season had finished, I would often go into town on a Saturday afternoon to meet up with the lads. We would also go in Jenny's Bar in the Britannia Hotel, where it would be a pound a pint.

Obviously Hotshot, the Galleys and all the other lads who we knocked about with were hooligans, but I never really went out with the intention of getting involved in that. That wasn't my main purpose: I loved the football side but also enjoyed meeting new people from all walks of life and having a buzz, which believe me we did.

I went to almost all the home games and, even if I wasn't going to the game itself, I was guaranteed to be in town on match day. It wasn't always possible for me to go to the away games for financial reasons, and I wouldn't go anywhere with the intention of jibbing — although if an opportunity did arise then I'd obviously take it. The ICJ would pay for nowt and go on the graft, but that wasn't my cup of tea. I didn't want to get a criminal record and I never got arrested.

I've been to a few grounds in my time, including Anfield, Elland

Road, The Den, Upton Park, Highbury, Hillsborough and St James Park. I've had a few trips to Wembley as well. Being in other cities when it kicks off can be scary if you don't know where you're going. If it went off in Manchester, I always knew where I was and could get home alright. United didn't get run that often but you never knew what could happen. I never ran, which could be problematic – it wasn't because I was hard as fuck or owt, it was simply because I can't run!

I remember a few hairy moments in the 80s at Old Trafford, in particular Everton around '86. It was winter at the time and it got dark after the match, which created a really moody atmosphere. We had marched back into town and around ten of us were approaching Deansgate when a big firm of Everton appeared from out of nowhere. There were about 40 of them and the United lads got off on their toes, but I just carried on walking. The next thing I knew, I heard a thick Scouse accent saying, 'Alright there, girl? Where's your boys gone?'

I looked to my side and there was a massive, six-foot-two guy there.

'They've got off, ain't they?' I replied, flashing him a smile and carrying on walking.

'So how come you ain't run then?' asked the Scouser.

I just looked at him and shrugged my shoulders.

'Because I can't,' I said. This broke the ice and got him laughing.

'I've just slashed one of your firm across the neck,' the big guy told me. 'It was a nigger.'

'Well done,' I replied, not knowing whether he was having me on or not.

I ended up walking right up to the end of Deansgate with the Everton lads, talking about the price of bread and the weather. I then said my goodbyes and doubled back to the pub. When I got there, I found out that a black lad from Birmingham who came with us had been slashed. I'd had a narrow escape.

When United played away and I wasn't going with them, I'd still *go into town for a beer and often saw a few of the Young Guvnors about the place. I knew a couple of them from where I lived so they were usually okay with me. When we played at home and couldn't afford to go into the match, you could guarantee we would still be at Old Trafford, hanging about the forecourt. We would wait around to see if anything went off, especially if it was a big game against a rival team. Most of the time it was more handbags-at-dawn than fighting. There was a lot of bouncing about the place and shouting, 'Come on, let's have it!'*

Sometimes we would drink bottles of cider and smoke spliffs behind the Dog & Partridge until three-quarter time, when they opened up the gates and we could get in to see the end of the game. At that point, we would bounce in singing and shouting as if we'd been there for the entire match.

From the 70s onwards, fashion also became a keen interest. I knew that what you wore was important from knocking around with my brothers and their mates, who were always talking about Fred Perry t-shirts, Perry belts, Lois jeans and Dunlop Green Flash trainers. Clothing had always been a big thing for me as well: I can remember being over the moon when I got my first pair of Adidas Kick trainers while still at primary school. It was handy having older brothers because, whenever they went out, I could raid their wardrobes, don brand new Lyle & Scott and Pringle jumpers and pretend that they were mine.

The atmosphere surrounding football was something else. Everybody enjoyed the buzz of the game, but nowadays I find Old Trafford to be soulless. The working-class culture has disappeared and been replaced by the corporate crew. There is no passion, no adoration and no love anymore. The times I knew and cherished are now of the past.

14
The Sweaties

Scarlet is living proof that you can't judge a book by its cover. A lot of people might have automatically labelled a girl as somebody who shouldn't be at the football, but we knew her better than that. I could see why she raised some eyebrows though, because there were matches where even the biggest, burliest bearded blokes were unable to take the heat. One of these was the England–Scotland game that took place at Hampden Park towards the end of the 80s.

As I've said before, we had no interest whatsoever in fighting for our nation because we always put club above country. Mobs like Chelsea, West Ham and Bolton loved to band together to take on foreign teams, but the only reason any of our lads went to internationals was to have it with other English mobs. All the other firms would try and take us out but none of them were capable.

This particular game was more than just your standard England v. Scotland match because a couple of years earlier, West Ham had teamed up with the Young Guvnors and attacked some of our lads, which had us itching for revenge. We knew the ICF would be there because the Cockneys are proper into the England scene, so we made up our minds that we were going to hunt them down and do them.

One of our frontline fighters at the time was a lad called 'J'. He grew up in one of the city's roughest estates and soon became a top United face. He has a better recollection of the game than I have because I was a little the worse for wear that day. This is what went down during the epic battle of the nations:

HOTSHOT

J

At 6.30am, between 70 and 80 of us travelled up to Glasgow on the train. We were looking forward to the day because it was quite hot and there was the promise of some good fisticuffs. Upon arrival at the station, we saw 20 Young Guvnors waiting to ambush us. They had made their way up there on overnight coaches. As our main faces went through the ticket barriers, one of the Guvnors had the audacity to say, 'Outside, United, now!' We followed him and his mates out of the station, but by the time we got through the exit the jokers had vanished into thin air.

We then set off to find a boozer and noticed that, although it was still early and there weren't many other lads about, there were loads of CID knocking around, staring at us and acting very Taggart-like. They were about as subtle as a hard-on in a leotard. The lads soon found a bar and we had a few drinks while we waited for another 50 boys to arrive. They were coming down on a coach run by a lad called 'M', but this was in the days before mobiles so it was potluck whether we would all end up coming together.

After a couple of pints in there, we moved on in the direction of Hampden Park with our CID escort in tow and noticed a mob of between 40 and 50 lads on collision course with our firm. This caused the police to panic but, as we drew closer, we realised that it was only M and his coach and so we incorporated them into our mob.

The day was heating up and we were starting to get the Old Bill worried. They began to harass us so we headed for a nearby boozer. There were 50-odd Chelsea inside, who all seemed pleased to see some fellow Englishmen. A bloke wearing an England shirt said, 'Who are ya?' and I replied 'Man United.' The fella's face immediately dropped but, luckily for him, his little party weren't the sort of lads we usually looked for so nothing went off. They were mostly barmies and United don't take liberties.

One drink later and we were off again. By this stage, our Lincoln

The Sweaties

nutters had hooked up with us and we were getting towards the 150 mark, which meant we were now ready to rock. We headed towards a shithole area of Glasgow and found a boozer with the top knocked off, looking more like a shack than a pub. It was ideal because it faced a huge grass verge, which was the perfect spot for downing bottles of Pils and enjoying the 70° Fahrenheit summer sun. We also had a pub full of Jocks for entertainment. They sang an impressive variety of anti-England and anti-poll tax songs that had us in hysterics.

At around 2pm, we left the pub and headed towards Hampden Park. We were fuelled up on lager and lusting for some payback. The Jocks weren't really on our minds at that moment in time, although maybe they should have been because the road was slowly filling up with them. The nearer we got to the ground, the more Jocks appeared. Some of them got brave and came over shouting the usual anti-English bollocks. Quite a few of them pushed their luck and ended up getting decked.

As we drew nearer to the stadium, we bumped into some bloodied-up Forest fans who warned us that there were hundreds of Jocks at the top of the road and that they were all 'casuals', as they called them in Scotland. The Sweaty Socks were apparently spanking any English that they saw. United's top lad said, 'Get to the back. We're carrying on!' and the Forest boys did as they were told.

After another 100 yards, we saw some bloodied-up Stoke lads who'd been attacked by the same firm of Jocks. Our top lad told them the same thing he'd told the Forest boys and they went to the back of the mob. When we finally saw the Jocks, it was a sight never to be repeated at a football match. There were between 400 and 500 of them in a semicircle in front of six mounted Dibble. They looked like the modern day equivalent of a scene from Braveheart. We had about 200 lads at this stage because of all the stragglers we'd picked up. As soon as the Sweaties saw us there was a huge roar and the sky filled with missiles. I could see how the Forest and Stoke lads had got bloodied up. But when

141

we rushed towards the Jocks they backed right off, leaving some of their fallen who tried to crawl under cars to escape.

'We're going straight on!' barked our top lad as we pushed forward. Then the cavalry came to the Scotsmen's rescue in the form of the Dibble, who steamed into us on their horses and forced us up a street to our right. They had obviously expected us to be cannon fodder and weren't too pleased at how the situation had turned out.

The road we were on led to Hampden's giant forecourt. A few of us earwigged a conversation that some nearby Old Bill were having and heard them plotting to send us across in ones and twos. Sure enough, five minutes later the police formed a two-metre-wide human corridor and made us walk through it in single file, while we got abused and gobbed on by the sea of Jocks on either side.

We eventually made our way into the ground and settled down to watch the match. I went off to see if West Ham were there in numbers, noticing a few of Derby's DLF knocking about. I'd met them at Old Trafford in April and taken them to Salford Quays after we played them because I knew one of their main lads. We soon got chatting and, partway through our conversation, it became apparent that they were stood near Forest's firm, who we had a big row with in the FA Cup quarter final at Old Trafford earlier in the year. One of the Forest kids starting giving it the big 'un, saying that they'd fought their way out of OT. I also talked to a small group of Millwall lads and found that there were only two West Ham boys present.

England won the game 2-0, with a goal from Steve Bull sending a nearby group from Wolves wild. Nothing of note happened off the pitch. There was a fight between Newcastle and Sunderland at halftime but that was about it. The Young Guvnors were hiding at the bottom right-hand side of the terrace and they didn't want any.

I told our top lad what Forest had been saying and let the boys know there were only small numbers of West Ham, which pissed them off a bit. We left together after the match and went to meet up with the lads who didn't have seats or hadn't bothered going into the game. We soon split up from the main group of England and walked through some moody estates towards the town centre. There were only a few Old Bill on the scene and no rival lads tried anything, although some Scottish fans did yell abuse at us. The area nearer to the centre would be a different kettle of fish, doubtless crawling with Scottish hooligans.

As we made our way up the side of the River Clyde, we noticed a biggish mob of lads with about five coppers in tow. We slowed down to a snail's pace to allow them to cross the bridge and get in front of us. Lo and behold, it was the Forest lot. We moved right in behind them. One of our lads said, 'Remember me from Old Trafford?' and then smacked a Forest lad, which set us all off. There was limited police protection for the Forest lot so they ran for their lives. A mob of Jocks was on the street opposite us at the time and had us running down the side streets soon afterwards. It was now an England v. Scotland situation and mayhem ensued for a few minutes, until the Old Bill regained control.

The police put us in a big square and tried to keep us there until our trains arrived. Some Derby lads told the OB that they'd travelled to Glasgow in vans and pestered to be allowed to go back to their vehicles. The OB eventually relented, so 40 of us blended in with the DLF and slipped away into the centre. We hung about until the last train home and had a few minor scuffles with some young Celtic lads. They threw some bottles and glasses at us from afar but that was really it.

The Manchester Old Bill were waiting for us at the station. They put us on our train and then produced a big, black liner filled with beer and ice, dishing drinks out to us. The officers took their hats off and sat chatting with the boys, laughing and joking about the day's events.

We never really took to England games because it wasn't our thing, but our appearance in Glasgow ensured that other firms thought twice about taking liberties. Those who might previously *have considered it knew now that we were likely to turn up for revenge. If they were smart, they decided it wasn't worth the bother.*

'The violence of a minority of soccer fans has smeared the name of football yet again,' announced a reporter for BBC News in the aftermath of the game. 'Strathclyde police had been tipped off that hundreds of English supporters were heading to Glasgow for the sole purpose of causing trouble. They were shadowed for three miles from the city centre to Hampden Park, yet some were still prepared to become involved in running street battles with Scots fans. Police intervened quickly. Arrests soared to over 100.'

United never gave a fuck about the 'Scots fans'. We didn't go to the game to represent England; we represented Manchester. We tanned the Jocks but, more importantly, we also tanned our bitter rivals Nottingham Forest, which taught them not to run off their mouths. It's a pity we didn't get to do West Ham as well, but you can't have everything.

15
More Mayhem

Nobody expects to go to an England v. Scotland match and witness a completely peaceful game. There are certain fixtures we would go to where we knew full well there was going to be trouble, and these were the ones we looked forward to the most. Then there were the towns and cities that took us totally by surprise. Bournemouth was a classic example. We travelled there thinking we'd be able to bowl around the town as if we owned the place and ended up having to defend ourselves against attack. Bournemouth's team didn't even have a firm back then, so we'd assumed there would be no chance of a row. What we didn't bank upon was a firm of Scousers turning up unannounced.

We spent the night before the match drinking and taking whiz in the Cyprus, which meant we were all a little worse for wear by the time our coach arrived. It took a good five hours for us to get to our destination, so we kept ourselves entertained by singing songs and taking the piss out of each other. The minute we arrived in Bournemouth, we headed for a boozer in the neighbouring town of Christchurch. I couldn't even begin to tell you what either Bournemouth or Christchurch was like, because by that stage I was too far gone to take in any of the sights. As far as I'm aware, they were both pleasant little seaside towns.

We were just settling down to drink our pints when I heard an angry cry of 'Munichs!'

'Who the fuck is this?' I yelled.

The nearest city with a mob was Portsmouth and that was

a good hour's drive away. We were scratching our heads, wondering which firm we were up against, when a 20-strong mob of casually-dressed lads came running through the door. We were straight into the fuckers, slapping them about the place without knowing which team they supported. After hearing them repeatedly using words like 'la' and 'kidda', it became apparent that we were dealing with a firm of young Scouse scallies. They had been on a grafting expedition to Bournemouth and decided to pay us a visit while we were in town.

A load of different thieves and conmen targeted Bournemouth, Torquay and Newquay because they were perceived as easy places to graft. I suppose they must have been less on-top for jibbing because they all have relatively low crime rates. Whatever the reason for the Mickeys choosing Bournemouth, their boys were no match for United. They were on their toes the minute it kicked off.

'The fucking little knobheads,' one of the other United lads grinned. 'We showed those dirty Scouse cunts a thing or two.'

It was always nice to do another firm at a game where we didn't expect much action. We were buzzing about our result, so we decided to carry on drinking at the pub to celebrate and fuck-off going to the ground. After a couple of hours of heavy boozing, we headed off to our coach to start the long journey back home.

'Hey, can you stop off at an off license so that we can top up on beer?' somebody asked the driver partway through the trip.

'Yeah, go on,' he told us. 'I can't see the harm in that.'

Had the driver known we were going to have the offy over he might have thought twice. All of the older lads loaded up on whisky while we nicked a load of beer and Coca-Cola. We ended up swapping some of our Coke for whisky as the older firm had lifted so many bottles that they didn't know what to do with them all. By the time we arrived back home in

More Mayhem

Manchester, we were completely off our heads. It was a perfect ending to a perfect day.

Bournemouth was a great weekend. We had a decent piss-up and a row, which is all that you can ever really ask for. I've got to give it to the Scousers for bringing it to us like they did: there aren't too many mobs that will go looking for it miles from their home city, when their team aren't even playing.

There might have been the occasional game that took us by surprise, but there were just as many matches where we expected to come up against stiff competition and ended up going home without so much as a punch being thrown. This happened when we played Millwall at their place. It was a major disappointment.

In 1849, a letter written to a London newspaper by a social researcher called Henry Mayhew had complained of conditions in an area of south London that could only be described as a slum. 'The air had literally the smell of a graveyard, and a feeling of nausea and heaviness came over anyone unaccustomed to imbibe the moist atmosphere,' he wrote. 'Not only the nose, but the stomach told how heavily the air was loaded with sulphuretted hydrogen; and as soon as you crossed one of the crazy and rotten bridges over the reeking ditch, you knew, as surely as if you had chemically tested it, by the black colour of what was once white lead paint upon the door posts and window sills, that the air was thickly charged with this deadly gas.'

The district that Mayhew found so unpleasant to enter was in a notorious shithole known as Bermondsey, where Millwall's ground now lies. Although no longer home to clouds of poisonous smog, it is still a rough and ready area where most of the locals look like extras from an East End gangster film. Travelling to The Den is like going into the heart of Salford's Ordsall estate or one of the most hardcore, blade-infested areas of Liverpool. It's a shady-as-fuck part of town and the local nutters always turn out in force.

You would have thought this meant the Millwall boys could always be relied upon to defend their patch. But you would be sorely mistaken, because they bottled it and pissed around until the Old Bill showed up.

On the day of the match, a thousand-strong mob of Red Devils marched through the streets of south London into the heart of Milwall territory, which must have been a sight to behold. We were closer to an army than a football mob. It was the Dibble's worst nightmare. They shut down all of the local pubs in an attempt to prevent it from going off, but all their actions did was force us further into our rivals' manor. We were hoping there would be somewhere closer to the ground where we could get a drink.

As we drew near to the stadium it became apparent that the Old Bill were planning on herding us into The Den, so 400 of us veered off into a nearby estate. We managed to avoid the Dibble long enough to get to the Old Kent Road, the street that divides Bermondsey from the neighbouring districts of Peckham, Camberwell and Walworth. All of these are moody parts of London, where an unsuspecting football fan can easily come unstuck. But then again, United aren't your average football fans – if anybody was going to get done it was unlikely to be us.

One of the lads suggested going into a nearby shithole pub. It was rundown and dilapidated, with a distinctly cockney feel. More importantly, it was one of Millwall's boozers. We were sure to get a row in there.

'Yeah, let's go in their watering hole,' another lad agreed. There were some Old Bill in the boozer, but they seemed more concerned with slagging Millwall off than keeping a lid on things.

More Mayhem

'Last season those cunts got promoted and they still went on the rampage!' an angry Dibble ranted down my ear. 'They were turning police vans over and smashing the place up. I'm glad you're here to give it to 'em. They're all in a pub on the other side of the park. They'll be pissed off that you're in their boozer.'

'Right,' said one of the boys. 'We'll have a couple of pints in here and then we'll go and pay the Millwall lads a visit.'

We were planning on bowling our way across the park and storming Millwall's pub, but a group of Old Bill caught us partway through our journey, escorted us to the ground and herded us inside. We got a few whacks with a truncheon along the way but it beat getting a charge sheet.

The game itself was proper boring. It was a goalless draw and I couldn't wait for it to finish so I could have it with Millwall's Bushwhackers. The minute the final whistle blew, we made our way up to the top exit gate and started rocking it back and forth. The Old Bill were eventually forced to let us out because they didn't want any damage done to the gate.

'You've got a choice of where to go from here,' a Cockney Dibble told us as we left the ground. 'You can either go left to the train station or right to the coaches.'

It was looking as if the police were leaving people to their own devices once they'd told them which direction to head in, which was a major error on their part. We opted to go left then made our way back to where Milwall's boozer was, to see if they were about. Sure enough, there were a couple of hundred Cockney thugs there, mobbed up and ready for it. They started advancing down the street towards us so we carried on up to meet them.

We had a good 800 lads with us. The moment the Bush-whackers realised what they were up against, they slowed down. They got to around 20 yards away from us and then stopped dead in their tracks, clearly having second thoughts about taking on a firm our size. I was proper gutted that they were bottling it as I'd been expecting the biggest pitched battle of my life. The Old Bill took advantage of the pause in proceedings and quickly put us in an escort. Our chances of a riot had now been well and truly dashed.

The OB marched us all to New Cross tube station and then hung about at the platform until our train arrived. If they'd wanted to prevent us from having another go at Millwall they probably should have nicked us, because we got off at Surrey Docks in nearby Rotherhithe and started marching back.

By this stage, the Old Bill were really not impressed. They decided to let out their frustration by leathering us with their truncheons, which caused one of our boys to retaliate by squirting an officer and his dog with an ammonia-filled Jiff lemon squeezer. This put the coppers on the warpath. They couldn't have us taking the piss like that, so they forced us to file past them while they set their dogs on us. Once they'd had their fill of brutalising us, they took us back to the tube station and shoved us on a rattler.

Imagine our delight when we saw a group of five young Millwall lads in our carriage. Their faces went white with terror the minute we caught their gaze. Fortunately for them, the Old Bill were on hand to escort them off the train. We would have given them untold amounts of shit if they'd stayed on board.

All in all we'd had an entertaining day out, despite the Five-O's attempts to ruin our fun and Millwall's arses going. We got to bowl around south London in a thousand-strong mob of Reds, which gave us all a major rush. My only regret is getting off the train at Surrey Docks, as I later found out that 100 Forest lads were waiting to ambush us at Euston. There were a thousand-odd United lads on the rattler, which would have had the Notts boys shitting in their pants. The looks upon their faces would have been priceless.

The Millwall boys are really nothing special. They aren't the worst mob we've been up against but they aren't the best either. For a team that hails from such a rag-arsed part of town, you'd think they'd be more up for it. Apparently nobody likes them and they don't care; well, maybe people would be more inclined to like them if they put a bit more effort into it.

Fortunately, there were teams that never let us down. Around about the same time we came up against Birmingham's Zulus mob, who were the firm that Millwall were hyped up to be. These lads were named after the largest ethnic group in South Africa, who fought bloody battles against British colonialists in the late 1800s. After chanting 'Zulu! Zulu!' for some unknown reason at a game against Man City in 1982, they'd decided that 'Zulus' would be a fitting label for their mob because they had a lot of black lads in their ranks. They were reputed to have a handy little firm, which made us curious to find out if they were as good as they were cracked up to be.

We were smoking weed and drinking cider at the Dog & Partridge in Old Trafford before a match one day when somebody suggested turning up unannounced to have it with the Brummies, who were playing Bury away. Their Zulu warriors were famous for violent toe-to-toes with Villa, but could they handle the Red Army? I suspected not.

We were in high spirits on the short journey to Bury, smoking weed and playfully taking the piss out of one another like we always did.

'We're going to fucking hammer those Brummie bastards,' one of the lads geed up the rest of the mob.

'Yeah,' I told him, 'those dirty Brummie cunts are going to get fucked up.'

HOTSHOT

United were playing Derby County, or Crystal Palace, or some complete wank which didn't interest me at all. Give me a tear-up with the Zulus over a boring game any day.

We bumped into the Brummies as soon as we got off the bus, which meant we got to have it with them earlier than expected. They were all a good few years older than our boys and looked confused by the fact that a load of teenage lads had turned up for a row. I didn't want them to think that we were Bury, so I introduced our firm.

'We're Man United. We've got a shit game today so we're here to do you in.'

With that the lads surged forward and started laying into them. Martin and me were the first two into the fray, launching ourselves at the frontline of Zulus. I got twatted in the face by somebody wearing a sovereign ring and the pattern was left imprinted on my skin. The Brummies seemed made up that somebody had turned out for them. They'd travelled down to Bury expecting a trouble-free game, only to be confronted by the monster that was United. It must have taken them completely by surprise.

We eventually got the Zulus on their toes but, just as they were backing off down the street, a load of Five-O turned up to put an end to things. The Old Bill had riot vans and canine units, which enabled them to regain control within no time at all. One of my mates got the pair of jeans he was wearing ripped to shreds by a dog, which was unfortunate seeing as another member of the firm had lent them to him.

'Oi!' the owner of the kecks shouted to the mutt. 'Get your fucking teeth off them, you cunt!'

The snarling beast paid him no attention whatsoever. It was time for us to make a move before we ended up going the same way as the jeans. We were disappointed that the action had come to an end but at the same time fully aware of what would happen if any of us got gripped by the Old Bill. They would realise that we had travelled into Bury specifically to have a row and no doubt throw the book at us.

'Well, we showed those Zulu cunts,' I said as I boarded the bus back home. We'd added another vanquished opponent to our increasingly large collection. Birmingham had lived up to their reputation but we'd done them all the same. It was time for us to hit the city centre and get off our heads to celebrate.

Our battle against Birmingham was a result-and-a-half, given that we hadn't even been playing them. It was the talk of our mob for weeks and had us eagerly looking forward to our next major row.

Although the Brummies were just as up for it as we were that day, there was another West Mids team whose lads were even gamer and harder. Birmingham had got a tidy little firm but they were no match for the club they shared a city with. Aston Villa were one of the best mobs in the country. They were always guaranteed to have a row and had some proper handy lads.

Fearsome as they were, they were yet another team whose end we invaded. When we played at Villa Park in the late 1980s, we went in their Trinity Road end and risked life and limb to prove ourselves.

On the day of the match, 40 of our younger lads got the train to Birmingham New Street. We had a couple of drinks in the pubs around the station before getting another train to Witton, where Villa's ground is. Witton is a rough-looking gaff filled with moody, rundown estates. It's little wonder Villa have got such a formidable set of lads because their manor looks like the type of place to breed proper lunatics. But they were still going to have their work cut out for them, whatever environment they hailed from. We were going to run them ragged in their own end and show them that they could bleed just like the rest of us.

As we drew close to the ground, I felt cool, calm and collected. I was comfortable in the knowledge I was surrounded by good mates. We would back each other to the death, which meant there was only so much damage the Villa lot could do.

'Okay, we're going for it,' one of the boys announced. 'Let's fucking do those Jasper Carrott-voiced wankers!'

Over the stile we went, heading straight into the belly of the beast. This was it, the moment we had all been waiting for.

As we walked across to the seats, a mob of 60 Aston Villa hooligans watched our every move from further up the stand. They charged into our lads as soon as we sat down, taking advantage of the fact that it's always easier to fight downhill than uphill. Their boys were a mix of different ages and races, unified by their desire to do us. They were incensed that we'd managed to gain a foothold in their territory and were intent on teaching us a lesson.

The Old Bill managed to break the scuffle up within a matter of minutes, but by that stage we'd already achieved our goal: the United boys had proven to Villa's mob that we were willing to take them on in their own backyard. We were thrown out of the ground, only to jib into our end again so that we could catch the remainder of the match.

'We did okay there, didn't we boys?' I grinned.

The other lads concurred. It was a good thing we'd seen some action off the pitch because the game itself was fairly uneventful. It finished up as a 0-0 draw and there were Old Bill crawling all over the place after the final whistle, making it impossible for us to have another pop at Villa. We eventually managed to slip away from the Five-O and headed into Aston for a celebratory drink.

The difference between United and a lot of the other firms

was that we had no reservations whatsoever about going for a pint in somebody else's manor. We didn't think twice about drinking in Aston, whereas very few other mobs would ever drink in our areas. Crews from out of town would go for a pint in City's manor but United were a different matter altogether. Drinking in Old Trafford on a match day was like signing a suicide note.

After hitting up a couple of the local boozers, we decided to get the train back home. We'd shown the Villa boys what we were made of and left our mark on their city, which meant our work in Birmingham was now complete. The United lads had notched up another victory and had a decent day out. It was time for us to party the night away in honour of our result.

Our scuffle that day was broadcast live on TV for the nation to watch. Home Secretary Douglas Hurd was present at the game and was commenting on how well behaved our fans were when we kicked off right in front of him. He rapidly changed his mind; I seem to recall him describing us as 'disgusting'.

Both of the Brummie mobs were formidable opponents, which is what you would expect from a tough city like theirs. They were similar to the Mancs in that they were diverse, multiracial crews from inner-city areas. There was one main difference though: the soundtrack to our riots. The Birmingham mobs were known for their love of reggae, especially the Zulus who walked around with ghetto blasters pumping out roots music. The Reds were always into tunes from closer to home though. With so much musical talent in our own backyard, we had no need to look further afield than Manchester for our sonic inspiration. First it was homegrown indie bands like The Smiths but then, towards the end of the 80s, a monster reared its head. Ecstasy hit the clubs and a sound evolved that catered to the chemical generation. Acid house was born.

16
The Acid House Years

Acid house was a musical subculture that developed off the back of the electro scene. A record executive called Morgan Khan started releasing early examples of the genre on his Westside Records label and its popularity in the UK grew from there. It was the music of choice for our firm because it was made by kids from estates similar to our own. None of the other working-class subcultures seemed relevant: punk had come and gone, as had ska in the Midlands, and hip-hop was more of a black-American thing. We finally had a sound that we could relate to. It was fast, it was hard and it was full of energy; what was not to like?

This innovative new genre was undoubtedly brought about by Ecstasy. I was fortunate enough to come of age in an era where pills were almost 100 percent MDMA. They cost £20 a pop but they were well worth every penny.

I was 16 when I took my first E and it was the biggest rush of my life. Adrenaline pumped around my body and my skin felt hypersensitive. Sounds were more vivid, women were twice as beautiful and everybody within a hundred-mile radius was suddenly my best friend in the world. It was the best buzz I'd ever had and there was no better music to take it to than the hard, relentless, throbbing beats that were emerging in the city's underground nightspots.

There are a lot of myths and legends in circulation about the Mancunian acid house scene, and the one that gets repeated time and again is that the Hacienda was the definitive venue. The truth of the matter is that it was shit. You had to be dressed up to the nines for the bouncers to let you through the door and it was full of posing bastards who spent the whole time trying to look cool. The best place in the city for acid house was a rundown nightclub in the heart of Miles Platting called the Thunderdome. The Hacienda only got recognised in around 1992, but the Dome was rocking from 1990 onwards. It was everything that the Hacienda was cracked up to be plus more.

The Thunderdome was also a focal point for hooligans from all over north and east Manchester. The majority of the ravers came from Miles Platting, Crumpsall, Ancoats, Newton Heath, Gorton or Beswick, but there were quite a few from Failsworth in Oldham as well. You had to have a smart shirt to get into the Hacienda but the bouncers at the Dome would let in anyone who paid. Everybody was accepted irrespective of who they were, with the only criterion for entry being that you had to be up for getting off your face.

There were always loads of City in the Thunderdome, but nothing ever kicked off with them because we were pilled up whenever we went in there. Remember the kid from Denton who hung me over the bridge in Chapter One? Well, now imagine me shaking his hand and dancing about the place with him. That's what the pills that were available during the 80s and early 90s were capable of. The little fellas weren't like they are nowadays, where people can take up to seven of them in a night. If you took that many Es in those days you'd be passed out on the floor.

A lot of the other ravers were into LSD. A type of acid tab known as a 'windowpane' would set you back a fiver; you could take half of it and get fucked. It was a cheaper alternative to taking Es, although I always preferred to do trips somewhere less full-on. If I was going to the Dome I had to have an E, no matter what it took to get my hands on one. Sometimes I'd rob from shops to get the money, at other times

The Acid House Years

I'd go to a club called Rotters on Oxford Street and steal the women's handbags while they were dancing.

Acid house came hand in hand with drugs; it was custom-made music for pills and trips. But the culture that was associated with it couldn't have been more different from your typical depressing drug scene. Taking Ecstasy at the Dome was as far removed as possible from going round to somebody's house, taking heavy drugs and laying back on the sofa all night. The buzz was upbeat and euphoric, with people dancing the night away as if they didn't have a care in the world. It was the perfect way to unwind without feeling under any pressure to pull a bird or have a row.

The one area where the Dome was slightly lacking was its physical appearance. It was a former bingo hall in the middle of a big, rough council estate. The inside consisted of a single large square room that got ridiculously hot to the point where perspiration rained down from the ceiling. It wasn't exactly the type of place where you were likely to rub shoulders with the rich and famous, but then again, who the fuck would ever really want to? The Hacienda was always full of stuck up B-list celebrities but everybody at the Thunderdome was down to earth. Nobody had an ego and everybody there was equal.

Although it was unable to compete with the Hacienda in terms of its location and layout, there was one area where none of the other clubs could ever touch the Dome: it had the best music in town. As well as spinning classic acid house records, the deejays played a genre called 'new beat' and even threw some completely unexpected tunes into the mix. One minute you would be listening to a darkly atmospheric techno track and then, the next thing you knew, De La Soul or Chaka Khan would be blasting through the speakers.

Jay Wearden was one of the most eclectic deejays at the Dome. His sets contained elements of everything from funk and soul to break-beat and hip-hop and he always knew how to rock a crowd. He talks here about the importance of the Thunderdome to the various scallies, thieves and hooligans that embraced the early acid house movement:

JAY

To me 1989 was definitely the year a social revolution took place in Manchester. It marked a change in behaviour for the working-class youth of the city, in particular the males. The acid house craze had broken out and Ecstasy was now the drug of choice. Onetime football hooligans and shady characters added dancing to their list of activities on a weekend, which had previously consisted of kicking the shit out of people. While there was still trouble in clubs, it was nowhere near the scale that we experienced in the early 80s.

People who were a part of this new culture were blown away. There was no going back for them. I never met a single person who said it wasn't for them. I suppose it brought about a sense of pure, carefree enjoyment without the hang-ups that accompanied a night out in the old, moody days of clubbing. These included copping off, the constant threat of violence and the pressure to look cool.

This was a new way of living and the Thunderdome totally encapsulated the acid house culture. It was full of some of the roughest ragtag geezers side by side with professional people. The club was built on word of mouth. There was no media coverage and very little in the way of promotion, yet each week it was filled with 1,500 sweaty lunatics having the time of their lives.

The venue's success was a complete accident because the owner, Alan Evans, had originally been struggling to run it as a rock club. It probably wasn't that far from closing when a local entrepreneur called Muffin started to promote Saturday nights there. It was an instant success, with the likes of JAM MCs, Steve Williams and the Spinmasters all playing. Alan and Muffin parted ways quite

Prowling the alleys
around Old Trafford. My
first ever football fight
was in these streets,
against West Ham's
infamous Inter-City Firm.
I was twelve years old.
© *Richard Milnes Photography*

In my pre-hooligan days, holding the FA Cup when it was on display inside the Scoreboard End at Old Trafford. I have supported the Reds since I was five years old.

BV the Master Dipper en route to Holland for a thieving spree in the early 1980s. The flick haircut is a giveaway to the period.

At the legendary Thunderdome club in 1989. Gangs from all over Manchester and Salford made it their home. It was rough but it was great.

Martin Gallagher, Fred, Andy and me getting out of our heads in Ibiza in 1989, during the peak of acid house. A lot of football lads of my generation got bang into the house music scene and all that went with it.

Boz, one of our party firm, getting bonkers in Thailand with Mani, bass guitarist with the Stone Roses. The Roses and the Happy Mondays led the way in the 'Madchester' era.

We had calling cards and badges made up in the mid-80s as a pisstake when all the other young firms took them seriously. The Jibbers got their name for bunking on trains and into matches without paying.

Phibby, on the left, and the notorious Eddie Beef, in the right, with a couple of fellow fans on a trip abroad. Beef is known to all as the 'King of the Jibbers'.

Despite the sheer size of our firm, we always knew you could come a cropper in the most unlikely places. Jeff's nose was split by a flying pint glass during a pub brawl before an FA Cup match away at Hereford United in 1990.

A gathering of United Youth in 1989 for my eighteenth birthday. From left to right: Ezza, Babba, Pete, Ged, Jimmy (JC) and Gilly.

Brooksy in my Gorton gaff after a night out at the Hacienda. He got himself on *Top of the Pops* with me and Eddie Beef when we appeared briefly on a Black Grape music video.

Celebrating United's first League title in twenty-six years with some of the younger United mob at the old Shambles Square in central Manchester. The square was wrecked by a huge IRA bomb three years later.

On that same memorable day in 1993, the mob from the Grey Mare pub in Miles Platting unfurl their flag in the square.

On the pitch at Old Trafford in a stunt put together by serial prankster Karl 'Fat Neck' Power. Karl is back left and Tommy Gunn is struggling with his Diego Forlan wig on the right. I am in the front row in the black shirt, the smallest goalie ever to appear at Old Trafford. © *Press Association*

Just to prove it wasn't all violence, United and Man City lads take a break together in Cyprus for the wedding of Bluey, a City lad. The group here were all good pals despite the football rivalry; this was our weekend drinking firm.

Anyone know the way to the ground? Larking about on a trip to Spain in 1994 to watch United in the Champions League

Made it: with the lads in Barcelona, just off Las Ramblas. We lost the game 4-0 to a Barca side that included Hristo Stoichkov and a rampant Romario.

Some of he lads stop off for an overnight in Milan on the road to Juventus. The big European away trips were always special.

A tasty Red Devils young firm holding up a United flag on a trip to Hamburg. As their flag says, 'MUFC ARE HERE. AS ALWAYS.'

Martin Gallagher's last battle: United versus Roma in 2008 saw clashes with Italian Ultras on the Old Trafford forecourt on Warwick Road. Many of the Italians had blades but seemed more interested in posing than fighting.

One of the lads, Danny, gives Mario Balotelli the two-fingered salute after the City loonball pranged his Maserati outside the San Carlo restaurant in Manchester. Fortunately there was a passing photographer to capture the incident! © *WENN.com*

The Men in Black on the night they turned up at Wayne Rooney's mansion in Cheshire in October 2010, demanding to know why he was reportedly planning to leave United. Rooney called the police – but stayed at the club.

Terrace legend Coco (left) gets his hands on the European Cup with me and writer and former grafter Colin 'Beaner' Blaney. © *Richard Milnes Photography*

Still partying: with Bez from the Happy Mondays, who was kind enough to a write a foreword for this book, and Galley at the launch of a terrace fashion book called *Dressers* in 2012.

With some of the lads: Phil Redmond, Beaner, Hotshot, Mikey and Robert Gallagher. © *Richard Milnes Photography*

quickly but Alan continued with the same line-up.

All hell broke loose one day when Cheetham Hill, a gang from North Manchester, decided to shoot the doors off the club. All of the DJs were warned not to play or the same would happen to them. There was presumably some kind of battle for control of the venue going on. I had just come back from Ibiza and heard about the situation. I rang the club and they were desperate for a DJ, so I was in. To play somewhere like that with so much passion was unbelievable. Every night was a pleasure. It was the polar opposite of the Hacienda. It wasn't cool to go to the Thunderdome in any shape or form; it was just fucking brilliant. Your whole life revolved around those nights and the kids from the rough neighbourhoods did what it took to get the money to fund their excursions to the Dome.

Jay wasn't the only acid house artist whose profile was boosted by the Dome; it helped to launch the careers of Mancunian deejay duo the Spinmasters, who went on to score a number of top 20 hits as part of a group called 808 State. Spinmasters deejays Darren Partington and Andy Barker have contributed a couple of statements on the origins of the club and the importance of football hooligans to the spread of acid house. Here's what they say about the venue that became a Mecca for music-loving footy thugs from all over the city:

DARREN

The Thunderdome was originally set up as a rock and heavy metal night by one of those rock 'n' roll types who dress in leather pants. It had a great sound system so we asked him if we could do an acid house night there, and he gave us a regular Thursday night spot. Friday and Saturday were reserved for the headbangers and leather-trouser wearers so we had to make do with a weeknight. We had access to a wide range of different tunes to play because we owned a record shop called Eastern Block in Manchester city centre, so the word about our nights soon spread. Before we knew it, estate kids from all over Manchester were travelling to Miles Platting to attend the Dome. It was a place where kids from council estates could unwind with people from a similar background. We played street music for street people and it was something that football hooligans could relate to, along with members of various other similar working-class subcultures.

Despite the fact that there were always a lot of hooligans present and it was in the middle of a rough estate, there was very rarely any trouble at the Dome. You could get a group of Reds at one end of the club and a group of Blues at the other and nothing would kick off. The rivalry between the firms was put on hold on a Thursday night. The clientele at the Thunderdome were far too heavily pilled up to even consider fighting one another; all they cared about was getting their heads down and dancing their arses off.

ANDY

Although the Dome was usually a place where beef was left at the door, there was still the odd spot of bother every now and again. One night somebody pulled up in a car outside the club, took a shotgun out of the back and peppered the bouncers with it. Another time somebody was firing shots around at the end of the night while we were waiting to get paid. We were playing pool inside the club when we first heard that somebody had a gun. One minute everything was quiet and the next thing I knew, everybody was screaming and running about the place.

'There's a guy outside with a fucking shooter. He's just shot the camera off the front door!' shouted a terrified passerby.

I couldn't see the point in abandoning our game just because there was a gunman knocking about the entrance. He didn't have any beef with us so what did we have to worry about?

The Acid House Years

'Look, he's not going to shoot the deejays is he?' I said to Darren. 'All we do is spin the tunes. Have your shot and we'll get off in a bit.'

We carried on playing pool until somebody won and then headed home.

The only other bit of trouble I can remember was when there was a minor altercation out the front and a load of coppers swarmed into the Dome. They congregated along the back wall, so we put on a song with a sample in it that said the word 'Babylon', the West Indian slang for the police. The minute they heard the tune the crowd turned around and started kicking off with the cops. It was fucking brilliant.

DARREN

None of these incidents involved the football heads. The two times when guns were used were towards the end of the Thunderdome's prime, when it started to get moody. Manchester's hooligans actually played an important role in popularising the type of music that we played. They travelled up and down the country to away games, spreading the word about acid house. One of our songs, 'Pacific State', was even played in the Stretford End before the matches; that's how popular we were with the football crowd.

Darren and Andy put Pacific State on as their last tune of the night whenever they deejayed at the Dome. They had A&Rs coming to the club just to hear that song, which was mad as fuck considering what kind of a gaff it was. It wasn't the type of place you'd expect a music executive to venture into; there was so much condensation in the air that clouds of thick white mist floated around the room, making it impossible to recognise anybody unless they were standing inches from your face. It's a little bit unnerving when somebody suddenly appears from the fog while you're off your head on drugs. I'm surprised nobody ever had a heart attack.

The nights at the Dome came to a close at 2am, at which point the ravers would pile out onto the streets, dripping wet with sweat and glowing like the Ready Brek kids from the heat. The Thunderdome was one of the hottest music venues I have ever been to in my life. It was like going to a rave in the centre of a volcano. You needed to take a change of clothes with you because you ended up so sweaty.

We were always high as kites by the time we finished at the Dome and usually went on to the Kitchen, in the Crescents area of Hulme, afterwards. The Kitchen started life as a recording studio and was originally run by a former university student whose mam was a barrister. The lad had tried his hand at putting on shebeens playing reggae but they always ended up turning moody. Just as he was considering downing tools and stopping his music events, Darren and Andy stepped in and asked him if they could deejay acid house at his venue. He agreed to their request and the Kitchen soon became another of our regular haunts.

When the occupant of the flat next door to the Kitchen moved out, the Spinmasters knocked the wall through to give themselves some extra space. They painted the entire venue black and put two little lights in the corner. The end result was two empty, dimly-lit, black-walled rooms crammed full of E'd-up football lads.

A couple of local Yardies kept turning up at the Kitchen, thinking that it still played reggae. They would stand and stare at the hordes of pill-taking white hooligans, wondering what was going on. The Yardies were reluctant to join in with us at first because they were used to Jamaican music, but after a while they became curious about the drugs we were taking and decided to try some Es. Within a matter of weeks we had them gurning their faces off in the middle of the dance floor, getting completely off their nuts. We were among the first people to introduce black lads from Moss Side and Hulme to Ecstasy. The mental image of a group of hardcore Rastas getting down to the Spinmasters will be imprinted on my brain forever.

We would also hit up illegal raves in Blackburn after going to the Dome. The organisers would break into a warehouse and set up speakers, decks and a mixer, converting the building into a makeshift acid house venue. Some of the events had up to 10,000 ravers at them, which was impressive given that they were advertised by word of mouth alone. The Hacienda? What the fuck was that?

There were similar illegal dance events in London but they had nothing on the raves up north. The lads who went to them seemed more interested in looking cool than having fun. None of the ravers at the Blackburn warehouse parties gave a flying fuck about their image. The crowd turned up for the music and the vibe rather than to come across as edgy or 'underground'. Nobody ever attempted to be anything that they weren't.

For the first nine months, the Old Bill had no idea how to stop the raves from taking place. There were so many people at them that it would have taken the entire Greater Manchester police force to bring them to a halt. Then, as the raves began to hit the news and embarrass the Five-O, the government came up with the Criminal Justice and Public Order Act, which included legislation specifically designed to prevent them from taking place.

The CJPOA gave the police the right to remove people attending or preparing for a rave, providing it was 'likely to cause serious distress to the inhabitants of the locality'. One of the checkpoints on the list of things that allowed the attendees to be removed read, '"music" [that] includes sounds wholly or predominantly characterised by the emission of a succession of repetitive beats'. Not only were they cracking down on raves but they snuck a sly dig at acid house into the legislation.

The Thunderdome's days were also numbered because naughty people were beginning to realise there was a lot of money to be made from selling Es at acid house events. Dealers were competing for control of the pill market and the loved-up vibe was quickly replaced by moodiness and fear. The venue was eventually shut down but its legacy lives on. It was one of the best nightclubs I've ever been to in my life and, although it lacked the fame and glamour of the Hacienda, those in the know will keep its name alive. Long live the Thunderdome: the one force on this earth that could stop a roomful of United and City from going at it. It is gone but not forgotten.

17
The Early 90s

Ecstasy may have made all our lads feel loved up, but another drug gained popularity towards the start of the 90s that did the polar opposite. Cocaine hit the scene in a major way at the dawn of the new decade and added new levels of aggression to the terraces. United never needed drugs to hype us up for a brawl though; we functioned purely off adrenaline. Coke affected us in a different way, transforming half of our mob into serious criminals. Shoplifters and lads who grafted swag at concerts realised how much money there was to be made from selling white and were transformed into dealers overnight.

The downside to the lads filling their pockets with drug money was that they were more wary about getting nicked at the football. When you're making thousands of pounds a week from crime, the last thing you want to do is put your freedom at stake for the sake of a punch-up at a match. This meant that some faces trailed away and our firm began to decline. Despite our fall in numbers I've still got some great memories from that period, one of the best being our away game at Hereford. It will always stick in my head, because we weren't expecting any trouble but ended up in possibly our most intense brawl to date.

Although it is the county seat of Herefordshire, Hereford is still relatively small, with a population lower than that of Gorton. It's a relatively upmarket town and has a pretty shit football club, so it's the last place on earth you'd expect anything to kick off. When we found out that we were due to play Hereford United in the FA Cup, we didn't think for a second that we'd end up having a row. We thought it was going to be one of the few occasions when we could watch the match without having to be on the lookout for rival lads.

Fifty of our boys travelled down to Hereford the night before the game to hit the local pubs. We spent the entire coach journey getting pissed and Charlied up, which was our regular routine whenever we played away. Coaches didn't come equipped with toilets back in those days so a bucket had to do. The contents would be thrown out of the window when the driver looked the other way, which can't have been too pleasant for whoever was behind us at the time.

Hereford is on the border to Wales, so it was no surprise to anyone that it was pissing it down with rain when we arrived. We got soaked through to the skin the minute we left the coach.

'Where can we go to get a drink?' our top boy asked a random passerby as we traipsed about the streets, attempting to find a watering hole. 'We're getting fucking drenched and need to find somewhere to dry off.'

'Don't go to the pub that I've just been past,' the fella told him. 'It looked rough as fuck.'

'Right,' grinned our lad. 'That's the pub we're going to.'

As we set off to find the boozer, the rain beat down even heavier than before. We pulled our hoods over our faces in a futile attempt to remain dry. It was proper fucking cold as well. I didn't care what pub we ended up in, just as long as it was warm.

When we eventually found the boozer, it was a large, old-fashioned gaff next to a military base. It was full of skin-heads and inbred hillbilly types, which is exactly what you'd expect from somewhere in the back of beyond like that. The atmosphere didn't seem too bad at first. It was only when the landlady came marching over and started kicking off that the situation took a turn for the worse.

'You're going to have to leave. You aren't welcome in here,' she told us.

What the fuck? We weren't doing anything wrong. She appeared to have taken exception to the fact that a large group of lads from out of town had come into her pub.

A heated argument ensued and, before I had a chance to calm the situation down, the landlady had picked up a chair and was advancing towards our boys with it. One of the lads lunged forwards and banged her out, causing the entire pub to go up.

'Have some of this!' yelled an angry six-toed yokel, launching a pint pot at our firm. Every drinker in the place seemed to want to join in, which resulted in a huge, Wild West-style brawl. I was only 19 at the time and some of the local lads were built like man-mountains. We were going to have our work cut out if we wanted to come out on top.

Partway through the row a load more drinkers came down from upstairs and piled into the fray. These boys didn't half know how to fight. There's an SAS base in Hereford, so I think a lot of them had probably received some form of military training. They were some of the toughest opponents I've ever come up against, which is saying a lot because United have had it with anybody and everybody. These lads were the business; they were hard as fucking nails.

As the fight progressed, the contents of a pool table were emptied and a volley of pool balls was exchanged. Some of the yokels ran out of the door and tried to come back in again, so we blocked the entrance up with tables to keep them out. By the end of the battle there were unconscious bodies all over the floor. None of the windows had any glass left in them and all of the chairs were overturned. It was as if the IRA had bombed the place.

I was so pissed up that I can't even remember how the fight came to an end. I'm surprised it ever actually finished because our opposition seemed capable of going on forever. For a town of its size, Hereford had some hard cunts living there. Out of our entire FA Cup run, our battle against the yokels was easily the most intense – although the game itself passed without a single punch being thrown. We beat the Hereford boys 1-0 and spent the remainder of the weekend getting pissed to celebrate.

Five of our boys ended up getting nicked that day. One of them was a fella called Corky from Miles Platting, who is adamant that the landlady engineered the situation so that we'd get ambushed by the lads upstairs. Here's his account of what went on:

CORKY

We set off to Hereford with the intention of getting some beers down our necks and watching our team. All I knew about the place was that it was a bumpkin town. Never in my wildest dreams did I imagine that the day would turn out how it did. The locals must have been looking for a scalp because they set us up good and proper. No sooner had we entered the boozer than the doors were locked and a load of big, hard army men came piling down from the top floor. They were built like brick shithouses, so there was no need for them to take us by surprise like that. It was a fucking liberty.

To be quite honest with you, I was shitting myself during that fight. We had to shield ourselves with upturned pool tables at one point. One of our Salford lads was on crutches, so I shudder to think what kind of state he ended up in. It wasn't the type of row that you'd want to go into with an injured leg. My best mate Jeff got caught by a flying pint glass, which split his nose in two. He was carted off to hospital in an army ambulance because the regular medical staff were all on strike.

Partway through the fight, one of the Hereford lads whacked me so I whacked him back and got nicked for it. For some bizarre reason, the Old Bill let me out the following day in time to see the match. They knew that I was there for the football so I've no idea why they didn't hold me until after it had finished.

The hospital staff told Jeff that the police were looking to have a word with him in the morning, so he discharged himself with his snout still hanging off. A copper saw him outside the ground and said, 'Are you the one who got his nose done in?'

'You're bright, aren't you?' Jeff laughed at him.

I spent the whole game getting stoned, which was just what I needed after an all-out riot like that. Jeff put in for compensation and got awarded six grand – but, unfortunately for him, he had a criminal record so the court reduced it to one. Now I don't know about you, but I'd rather have both sides of my nose than a poxy £1000. It was the ultimate piss-take.

So there you have it; a bunch of country bumpkins nearly cost a lad his schnozz and gave some of United's gamest lads a run for their money. They were doubtless looking to test their wits against a mob of our standing. I doubt they get much excitement round those parts, so it was probably the most exciting thing that ever happened there.

Our run-in with a pub full of Hereford commandoes was by no means our only surprise during that period. We also got a shock when Bolton turned a decent mob out for us because they usually don't show their faces. Their inbred, pie-eating lads are always going on about how much they hate us but, despite their claims that we're their biggest rivals, we've hardly ever seen the cunts. They've never come to Old Trafford and barely even show up on our radar.

Bolton are one of those mobs that like to suck up to other firms. They've spent far more time joining up with Chelsea at England games than fighting the team they claim to despise. This is probably because our Salford lads alone could tan their inbred arses. They may class us as their archenemies but we really couldn't give a fuck about them. I could probably name a hundred different teams that we have a bigger rivalry with than those arse-licking twats.

But, on the day of this match, 30 of our top lads boarded the train to Bolton in the hope that our so-called rivals would show up. We weren't expecting much from them. As we pulled into the station, I'd be lying if I said I felt particularly excited because we usually saw neither hide nor hair of them. We might as well have been playing a team without a firm.

None of us had tickets so we decided to give the game a miss and hit the pubs instead. We found ourselves a boozer fairly near the ground and settled down to get pissed. Twenty minutes into our drinking session, there was a sudden wave of noise and 60 angry Bolton lads came flying through the doors. These boys had come to do the business, which was surprising because we'd never had any trouble from their lot before. They seemed determined to make up for their previous absences.

Tables and glasses flew around the boozer as we went toe to toe with Bolton. It took a good ten minutes to run them out of the pub, which is a ridiculously long time for a toe-to-toe to last. We chased them out of the door and would've finished them off if the Old Bill hadn't arrived en masse as soon as we left the building. It was a shame because we'd have liked to give the Bolton boys more of a going over. We couldn't complain too much though, because we'd managed to have a row with a firm that we didn't expect to show, which had us all buzzing.

Although I don't rate Bolton at all, I've got to give them credit for what they did that day. The lads that had it with us at the boozer were all as game as they come and put up a fair bit of resistance. If they could do the same at Old Trafford then maybe they'd be worthy of our respect. As it is, they are a firm who like to slag us off despite very rarely making an appearance when our team play theirs. They should carry on firming up with other mobs because it's the only way they're ever going to stand a chance against United.

Bolton's buddies Chelsea were a different story altogether. They might have mobbed up with the likes of the pie eaters and gone around calling themselves 'England', but they were still a notch above their mates. Although they never did anything at Old Trafford, we could always rely on them for a scrap round their neck of the woods. They could pull impressive numbers and defended their turf until the end. Unfortunately, on the day that we were scheduled to play them, 30 of us travelled to their manor but lost track of the time and left it too late to go in the ground.

'Fuck it, let's carry on drinking here,' said our top lad. There was no point heading to the match because we'd already missed a hefty chunk of it.

After downing pint after pint at a pub near Stamford Bridge, we decided to go on to another boozer for a change of scenery. We were walking down the street when a cacophony of cockney accents filled the air and 200-odd Chelsea hooligans sprang out of nowhere. They were all fully-grown blokes in their 30s and 40s, which meant that we were up against fellas twice our age as usual.

'Nobody's running here,' said Martin. If we refused to budge an inch then we'd at least leave with our pride intact.

HOTSHOT

We kept our lads tightly packed so that we only received a couple of digs here and there. Everybody stood and fought, which was a result in itself, given how badly outnumbered we were. Chelsea were bang off and I can't fault them for their performance. Many weaker firms would have crumbled but United all stayed put.

After a good few minutes of us going at it, the Old Bill arrived on the scene and tried their hardest to get the situation under control. Chelsea initially carried on into us but there were soon too many officers on the streets for the violence to continue. I was disappointed that the action had come to an end but made up that we'd stood our ground. Now all that remained was for us to give the police the slip and have a celebratory drink.

We hastily left the area before the Dibble got a grip of us and made our way to the City of London for a night out on the piss. We were buzzing about the day's events and chatting excitedly to one another about the scuffle. The Cockneys might have had the numbers but United had the fighting spirit. Whether there were ten of us or 200 of us, we always had a go.

When we'd finally finished celebrating, we made our way to Euston station and boarded the last train back to Piccadilly. We were still in high spirits about our result and belted out football songs during the journey. The ticket inspector wasn't overly impressed.

'You lot are being too loud,' he said. 'I'm afraid I'm going to have to ask you to leave the train at the next stop.'

This was all we fucking needed. We were kicked off at Rugby, which is a good two hours drive away from Manchester. There were no more trains and it was 2am.

We ended up having to pay for taxis to take us the remainder of the way. It was a shite way to end the night but it failed to kill the excitement of our row. United had taken on a mob over five times our size and emerged unscathed.

The Headhunters might have been up for it that day, but it was very rare that anything would go off when we played them at home. I remember a match at our place where a couple of Chelsea lads were bouncing about United's forecourt, giving it the big 'un, and had to be taught a lesson. You can always spot a plastic hooligan a mile off. If they were really up for it then they'd have got bang into us without running off their mouths. They were blatantly trying it on so that they could tell their mates about it later at the pub so I decided to pull their cards.

''Ere are, watch this,' I told my mates, reaching down into the pocket of my coat as if I was about to pull a blade.

'Have some of this, you wanker!' I yelled, jabbing the nearest Cockney in the chest.

'Aargh!' he screamed. 'I've been stabbed!'

'I opened up my hand to reveal an empty palm. All of the other United fans bent over backwards laughing as the silly fucker realised he'd been tricked. We spent hours on end that day doing impressions of the fella. He shouldn't have given it large if he didn't know the difference between a finger and a knife.

The lad I took the piss out of that day wasn't one of the Headhunters' proper hooligans; he was a pathetic wannabe attempting to impress his mates by playing at being a thug. The main Chelsea faces were all as real as can be and still have a decent mob today.

18
Leeds

Our run-ins with the Chelsea lads were nothing personal; as far as we were concerned, they were just another firm to have a rumble with. The same could not be said of some of the mobs closer to home.

As I've already told you, Liverpool and Man City both despised us and Bolton classed us as Public Enemy Number One. Then there were those inbred hillbilly idiots Leeds United. For some unknown reason, they have always cursed the ground United walk upon. It's a completely one-sided affair because we've never really given enough of a fuck to hate them back. I've always been of the opinion that they should try to do something about it if they hate our team that much. It's one thing to slag off somebody, but it's another matter altogether to prove how strongly you dislike them on the terraces.

Much as it pains me to admit it, Leeds always had quite a decent firm. They were years behind in terms of fashion and their sisters were also their wives, but they had a few handy lads with them. They could be relied upon to pull the numbers, which I think is partly due to the fact their city only has one football team despite having quite a large population. This meant that all of the hooligans in Leeds were affiliated with the same firm, as well as lots of lads from the surrounding towns and villages.

To understand our rivalry with the Leeds boys, you have to look at the history of confrontation between two sets of supporters. The Yorkies have hated the Mancs for decades. There was a period in the 70s when they would run us ragged whenever our team played theirs, which seems to have made them think they stood a chance against us. A lad called Mark Blaney, from the Racecourse Estate in Sale, had just started going to the games at the time. He is the brother of Colin Blaney, the geezer who is writing this book for me, and witnessed the turning point when United first started holding their own against the Yorkie hordes:

MARK

Up until this game, the hairy-arsed Yorkies had terrorised us whenever we played them at their place. According to the lads who went to the games, Leeds regularly chased our boys for the four very long miles back to the station from their ground. Those Yorkshire puddings pelted our fans with bricks and pieces of concrete from a new motorway that was being built, moving in on anybody who was unable to keep up with the herd. If anybody got tripped up from behind then it was curtains for them.

This all changed on the day of my first trip to Elland Road in the late 70s. I went there with my brother Colin and the Collyhurst Crew, who were one of United's main firms at the time. This ragtag bunch of thugs and thieves was led by George Lyons, Mickey Farrell, Willis and Gaftney. They were there when United took the piss in the FA Cup semi at Hillsborough and took over half of the rival section, which shows you what they were capable of.

In the build-up to the game, an assortment of Newton Heath pickpockets gathered at Victoria Station and poised ready to relieve travellers of their valuables the minute they left the train. As the passengers stepped down onto the platform, hordes of thieves swarmed past them onto the carriages, dipping them as they went. The minute the coast was clear, the Reds got off again and waited for the next train to arrive. Grafting went hand in hand with the football. Ardwick, Gorton and Miles Platting were probably the sharpest at dipping wallets and arnies at the games. They would also snatch takings from snack bars, shops, pubs and turnstiles, and even taxed the hotdog sellers.

I stayed close to Colin all throughout the game because he needed me on hand to pass stolen money to. The fact that I was so young made me less likely to get searched.

'You're going to see something impressive after the game,' he told me at halftime. 'Stick with me and you'll be in for a surprise.'

Sure enough, after leaving the ground 200 of United's top faces started walking in the opposite direction to the train station. We followed them as they turned right at the pub, passed the chippy and headed up towards the coaches. Shortly after this, a war cry went up from Mickey Farrell, signalling for the lads to double back and ambush the Leeds fans. The pace picked up until it was a full-on charge.

'Let's have it, Leeds!' one of the boys shouted.

We steamed right into the heart of the Yorkies, which was perfect timing because they were almost on top of United's barmies. The police had expected to escort United on their usual route, so they were completely unprepared for an attack from the rear. The Yorkshire puddings got the shock of their lives as our boys went into them like a stiletto in the spine, twatting them all over and forcing them into the side streets. A certain lively lad from Wythenshawe really stood out that night. He pounded away and connected windmills into every Leeds head that came near him. A decade later, he would go on to become one of the main boys in United's firm. It was sweet payback for all the times the Yorkies ran us ragged while we were in an escort. Gone were the days of United getting on their toes; we were now the predators rather than the prey. The Old Bill eventually managed to get behind us and regain control, but by that stage we already had the day.

One of the reasons the Leeds lot had been able to terrorise us so effectively was that PC Plod and his mates deliberately planned it so that they could get at the Devils. It made sense really, because once

179

United were on the run the Dibble's job was done. The Old Bill never spared a thought for the scarfers who got maimed and mangled in the process.

My enduring memory of the game that day was a load of coppers with big, white globs of spit all over their backs. This was a regular occurrence back in the day. It would look as if a bird had shat all down the bastards' uniforms. I guess they got their just desserts.

Funnily enough, Leeds managed very briefly to regain their status as the better of our two firms during the early 90s, when they gave us a kicking at a night match at Elland Road. It was a short-lived victory because we repaid the favour at the following match, but it still shows they're no pushovers. We were determined to have a row without the Old Bill getting onto us, so we decided to travel down by car to throw them off the scent. We'd arranged to meet the older firm partway through the journey, with the intention of driving through Bradford into Leeds the back way. I knew a lad from Gorton who had a set of wheels, so I rang him up and persuaded him to give us all a lift.

Our driver assumed that we were playing at Old Trafford, so you can imagine the look on his face when we said we wanted to go to Leeds. J was one of the lads who travelled down with us and he has a better recollection of what happened after we arrived:

J

The first thing we did was plot up in a boozer and get a couple of drinks down us. We'd drunk at the same pub on previous trips to Leeds and never gave the landlord any grief or jibbed his fruit machines, so he repaid the favour by being sweet with us. We left the pub at around 6.30 and made our way towards the ground but partway there our lads became spread out, which left the boys at the back of the mob open to attack. The Service Crew capitalised on our mistake and charged out of a pub to pick the stragglers off. They took us totally by surprise and overwhelmed us instantly. A couple of our boys took some pretty heavy digs and I was hit with an umbrella.

To give them credit where it's due, the Leeds lads mainly stuck to using fists. If we'd been caught off guard like that by the Scousers then we'd have doubtless been cut up. That's the only positive thing I can say about the attack because we got the kicking of our lives. Some of the lads at the front of our mob attempted to run back down the road to help the boys at the back, but it was too little too late as the Service Crew already had the upper hand. They ran us all the way down the street until we got to the next road, where we were able to regroup as a mob again.

By the time we'd regained our composure for round two, the Dibble had formed a line in front of Leeds. A couple of lads from both sides managed to get past the Old Bill to have a pop at one another and there were a few scraps here and there, but it was basically all over. One unfortunate Yorkie came charging across to have it with us, only for somebody to trip him up and send him sprawling onto the tarmac. The dull thud when he hit the deck sounded like dropping a sack of spuds. He wasn't getting up again in a hurry.

The Old Bill escorted us towards a subway, which was a bad move on their part because herding a load of football thugs into a tight space is a recipe for disaster. There was a giant free-for-all and, by the time the Dibble had managed to restore order, there were unconscious bodies strewn across the floor. We had got a second round in after all.

We were eventually herded to the turnstiles at Elland Road and made to go in the ground. Our battle in the subway was the last row of the day because the Old Bill were on top of things by this stage. The day belonged to Leeds but we still had our FA cup match against them in seven days' time, which gave us a chance to redeem ourselves – and redeem ourselves we would!

The FA Cup is always guaranteed to bring old faces out of retirement. It also means bigger allocations and harder work for the Old Bill. The Dibble's heavy workload usually results in them giving the thugs a bit of leeway, so we knew we would definitely get a fight. It was just a matter of making sure that we were smarter and better organised than last time so that the Leeds lads couldn't run us ragged.

Between 250 and 300 of us met up at a spot around two miles from the ground, which was our usual rendezvous point in Leeds. We already had a really top-class mob and all of our main faces were in attendance. The Old Bill had no idea where we were meeting, so we were left to our own devices. This time we would be a lot more tenacious when dealing with our rivals. We knew that Leeds were likely to have been buoyed by their victory the previous week and would be expecting another win. They were going to get nothing of the sort.

We left it 15 minutes later than the previous week to head off to the ground and kept our mob packed tight throughout the journey. As we neared Leeds' pub, we stopped and waited quietly on the right-hand side of the road. Sure enough, a couple of minutes later their firm left the boozer and started making their way up the street. We crept silently up behind them and were into them before they realised we were there.

This time we were the ones who called the shots. The ensuing melee was similar to the previous week, but with the roles reversed. Leeds were taken completely by surprise and tried to fight a rearguard action, all to no avail. We still had the events of the last match imprinted in our brains, which made us all the more determined to even up the score.

As the battle intensified, the Old Bill started flapping like fuck. One of them ran along a wall filming the fight while his colleagues gathered Leeds into a mob. The riot police kept our rivals in position for us, which was the stupidest move imaginable. With nowhere to run to, the Service Crew felt the full force of United as we steamed into their boys. Fortunately for them, they were able to hurry through the subway during the chaos, which gave the Dibble the necessary space to get between both sets of lads. The OB prevented us from going any further until we were at a safe distance from our opponents.

'Good turn out tonight,' United's Football Intelligence Officer let onto me.

'That's the FA Cup for you,' I smiled back. I had a sneaking suspicion he was proud of us after seeing how we'd got our revenge.

Nothing else went off after the game. There were a few skirmishes near Leeds' boozer but no more major incidents because the Old Bill had it boxed off. We ended up finishing our day out in one of the nearby pubs, where the locals were having a quiz night. I was queuing for my first drink when a voice came across the PA system: 'Can the person who has stolen the clock off the wall please put it back?' I burst out laughing; we'd already ruined the poor locals' quiz and we'd barely got through the door.

I've got to give the Leeds lads credit for their initial victory. They are definitely one of the better firms that we've been up against, although their attitude leaves a lot to be desired as they've got a lot of bigots in their ranks. The Service Crew have a reputation as a racist mob and minorities are guaranteed grief round their way. A pal of mine called John knows this all too well, because he went there with a couple of black and mixed-race lads in the early 1990s:

HOTSHOT

JOHN

When we got to Elland Road that day there were a couple of dick-heads selling National Front booklets outside the ground, which was exactly what we'd come to expect at Leeds. The fans of teams from the back of beyond were always far more easily taken in by racist propaganda. United never really had a strong right-wing contingent; we left the BNP and the NF to the likes of Bolton, Oldham and Stoke. That type of thing proved a lot more popular in places where there were hardly any black people. Manchester was far too multiracial for prejudice to take hold.

'What the fuck does the NF have to do with football?' shouted one of our older lads, pushing the seller to the floor and scattering his booklets across the pavement. 'Go on, fuck off, you prick!'

Elland Road is a shady place for anybody who isn't white, even without the far right stirring things. The Leeds boys aren't exactly known for being the most inclusive firm. They have a reputation for singling out black lads, which is part and parcel of their bullying attitude. Their Service Crew firm have no qualms whatsoever about attacking kids and non-violent supporters; taking liberties is second nature to them. We had taken a mixed-race City lad along with us and we didn't need clowns giving him a hard time. He might have been a Bluenose but he was one of our good mates, which meant we had his back.

Our group decided not to go into the game because none of us had tickets. The Service Crew had plotted up at the station in the belief we would travel down by train, which meant they were nowhere to be seen. We were searching aimlessly around the ground for them when a couple of Leeds fans started coming up to our City mate, making monkey noises in his face. I wanted to smash their faces in but there were far too many Old Bill about.

'Right, anybody who doesn't have a ticket needs to leave the area immediately,' announced one of the Dibble.

This was the other officers' cue to split us up into smaller groups and

Leeds

send us on our way. It was looking increasingly unlikely that Leeds were going to show their faces, so me and the six lads I ended up with headed up the road to try and find a pub. Just as we were beginning to think a row was out of the question, 20 Yorkshire thugs came bowling round the corner and advanced along the street towards us. They were all dressed very similar to one another. They had Berghaus jackets on and looked like a set of dummies from an Ellis Brigham skiwear and outdoor clothing shop window.

The Yorkies may not have been the most original dressers but what they lacked in individuality they made up for in the intensity of their hatred for United. The situation wasn't looking hopeful; we were badly outnumbered and had no idea where the rest of our lads had gone. I had a feeling that we were about to come unstuck.

Our black lad knew full well that he'd be singled out and attempted to make a run for it. This proved to be a mistake because ten racist Leeds hooligans went tearing after him. The rest of us all legged it back towards the ground with the remaining Service Crew members hot on our heels.

The Old Bill weren't best pleased that we'd disobeyed their order to stay away. 'You can either fuck off down that street or I'm going to nick the lot of you,' a pissed-off Dibble told us. There were a load more Service Crew lads in the direction he was pointing in; he was putting us in a no-win situation.

'We would if we could,' I said. 'But trust me, we really, really can't.'

'You're going to end up in the cells if you stay here,' the copper warned me. 'You can either do as I say or I'm going to arrest you.'

We were left with no choice but to face the Leeds crew. As we did as we were told, walking along the street towards our rivals, I noticed they were all roughly the same age as us. We were used to taking on middle-aged blokes so it was going to be like fighting little kids.

'We'll get through this lot easily,' I said. 'I don't know what we were so worried about.'

The two groups readied themselves for combat and it went off proper.

HOTSHOT

Our lads quickly got the upper hand, leathering the Service Crew all over the street. Hotshot got one of the Leeds boys up against the wall and gave him the pasting of his life. We may have been outnumbered but we were far from outclassed.

Our rivals soon got on their toes, which left us feeling pleased at the way we'd managed to turn the situation around. Our initial nerves had subsided and we'd plucked victory from the jaws of defeat. Now all we needed to do was find the rest of our firm and we'd be sorted.

By this stage the match was just coming to an end, so we made our way back to the ground to see if any of the lads who'd gone into the game were there. There were still a fair few Old Bill about, so we told them we were only sticking around until our mates came out and they let us wait behind a line of vans and horses. This turned out to be the best place for us as a load of angry Leeds fans quickly gathered round. They were almost frothing at the mouth at the sight of us and seemed intent on doing us. Some of them even went as far as to try and climb under the horses' legs to get at us. The hatred that they had for United was unbelievable.

We were eventually reunited with the rest of our firm and made our way back to our cars. The majority of the Old Bill stayed at the ground, which shows you how different the policing at the matches was back then. Nowadays an army of Dibble would have escorted us everywhere we went. The weak police presence allowed us to head straight for one of Leeds' main pubs. Now that we had our full firm onboard, we were confident we could take on the entire Service Crew. It was time for mob-on-mob action.

The Leeds boys must have known we were coming because they had a huge firm ready. They were stood outside the pub and spared no time in getting into our lads. Some of them were armed with canisters of teargas, which left our eyes stinging like fuck. It was going to take a lot more than that to save them from United though. We would show those inbred fuckers

Leeds

hatred — they didn't know the meaning of the word.

Bemused straight-goers looked on in amazement as fists and feet went flying. Leeds were no match for our firm and struggled to remain afloat. A couple of their lads got knocked out, which caused the rest of them to panic. They eventually lost their bottle and legged it down the street with us in hot pursuit. The Old Bill turned up en masse before we had a chance to catch up with the Service Crew. It was getting majorly on top so we decided to call it a day. We'd done what we set out to do.

The Leeds lads might have been as racist as they come, but they were still an undeniably good firm. There is no point slating them just because they claim to hate us so much. It's just a pity they so rarely turned their hatred into action and actually did us. Still, they gave us a few close shaves — which is more than can be said of most firms, so kudos to them for that.

19
Adventures in Paddyland

Bigoted as Leeds were, their team at least hailed from a multicultural city. An area called Chapeltown in the north east of the town was their equivalent to Moss Side, with a large West Indian population and lots of Rastas, which meant that even the most hardened racists came into contact with minorities at some point. The same could not be said of Dublin, where Galley went to watch England play Ireland during the same period. Not only did the locals hate anybody with a darker shade of skin but they were also militantly anti-English, still harbouring a grudge because of their ill treatment throughout history at the hands of the Brits.

This particular game was similar to the England–Scotland match in that it attracted a fair few lads who wouldn't usually have turned out for an international. They weren't arsed about England though – they just wanted to have a day out on the piss. Here's Galley to tell you how our boys got on in the land of leprechauns and Guinness:

GALLEY
Although I usually wouldn't bother following the national team, I made an exception for this game because I thought that it might be a laugh. Fifty of our older lads and ten of the younger firm were going, so I knew I'd be in good company. As luck would have it, there were also three young Mickeys called William, Garry and Christie on the boat across, who'd given us heaps of shit throughout the years.

Whenever we bumped into their mob all we ever heard was 'Munich this' and 'Munich that', so it'd be interesting to see if they behaved the same way when they were surrounded by our boys. It's easy to hurl abuse when you're in the middle of a mob, but when you're stuck on a ferry with a group of 60 rival fans the temptation tends to be a lot less.

Partway through the journey, one of the Scousers came to ask for my help because the older United lads were giving him pure abuse.

'Look lads, I know we've had our shit in the past but we're all England today,' he grovelled, adopting a creeping tone to his voice that made me feel slightly nauseous.

'Fuck off, you little Scouse cunt. We're going to throw all three of you over the side,' I told him. It was proper stormy and the boat was rocking all over the place. It really wasn't a very good day to take involuntary swimming lessons.

The word began to circulate that the Scousers were going overboard and they started whimpering and pleading. 'Look, Galley,' one of the miserable bastards whined to me. 'It's only youse that can help us. It doesn't have to be like this.'

I couldn't help but feel a little bit sorry for him, so I decided to have a word with the older United lot. 'The Mickeys aren't firmed up,' I said. 'By all means abuse 'em and give 'em shit, but if anything's going to happen us young 'uns will give it to 'em.'

The older lads agreed and continued to wind up the Scousers for the rest of the journey. None of us laid a finger on them but we constantly made out that we were going to, which served them right for all the times they'd shouted 'Munichs' at us over the years. If we'd been stuck on a ferry with a load of Scousers then we'd undoubtedly have been done. Fortunately for them, United don't take liberties.

The minute we reached dry land, we piled into the port and had a look about for a boozer. It's always good to start the day how you mean to carry on. We found a decent enough watering hole and I went on the fruit machines while the rest of the boys drank their pints. By the time I'd finished frittering away my money, the pub had completely emptied and I was left on my own. I had no idea where I was going so I set off in search of United.

I was wandering the city when I saw three Wigan lads from the boat, who asked me if I wanted to go grafting with them.

'Go for it,' I told them. 'Let's get to it, then.'

The Wigan boys chose a mountaineering store because it sold expensive outdoor clothing that was easy to sell on. The minute we entered the shop, two of them started asking the assistants a barrage of different questions while the third picked up a rack of Sprayway coats. He quickly sprinted out of the door with it, with the staff giving chase. It was time for me to get off.

After being chased around the streets for what seemed like forever, we eventually managed to dart into a pub and hide. We stayed there until the situation was a little less on-top, then we made our way to the area near the ground to sell the coats on to the locals.

Dublin is quite a racist city and a couple of our potential customers didn't take too kindly to a mixed-race kid approaching them, but the Wigan lads immediately jumped to my defence.

'Look, it's not about all that,' they told the Paddies. 'Do you want to buy a coat or not?'

The locals eventually calmed down and we headed off to the stadium before more trouble came our way. None of us had tickets but, fortunately, a bluenose called Daft Donald was on hand to kick open the gate. Donald was always doing crazy things like that. Daft as he may have been, we probably wouldn't have got into the game without him so I'll give credit where it's due.

The second the gate was open, a swarm of England fans steamed into the ground and it went mental with the Paddies. Punches and kicks rained down on me from every direction and I was soon covered from head to toe in claret. The Irish Old Bill were on the scene within a flash and quickly separated the mobs. They shoved

HOTSHOT

me over with the rest of the United fans and I breathed a sigh of relief that I was finally reunited with the boys.

Our troubles with the Paddies had only just begun though. We were walking into Dublin city centre after the game when William, Garry and Christie came tearing down the street, yelling, 'Fuckin' run, Galley, it's on top 'ere lad!' I looked behind them and there was a huge firm of Irishmen haring down the road. Luckily, the Man U mob hadn't got too far so I had back-up there. Before I knew it, we were scuffling away with the Paddies as if there was no tomorrow. One of the Irishmen had his denim jacket snatched from off his back; it had a big ink stain on it but the lad who taxed it was still chuffed as fuck.

The Old Bill eventually got a grip of things and started herding us to the ferry port. Unfortunately for them, there was also an IRA supporters' march going on nearby and a group of angry Irish Republicans started throwing whisky bottles over the top of our police escort. Pieces of broken glass rebounded off the pavement as the Paddies expressed their hatred for the English the only way they knew how.

A few of them managed to somehow sneak around the Dibble and tried to drag me off. I assumed I was being arrested at first and was reluctant to fight back. Then, when I realised I was being kidnapped, I started punching my attackers as if my life depended on it. Looking back, it might well have done. I don't know if they were fully fledged IRA or just sympathisers, but they definitely looked as if they meant business. Luckily, a couple of our younger lads stepped in before the situation got too serious, pulling me out of the Irishmen's grasp and dragging me to safety.

Well, *I thought to myself,* the fucking IRA! That's a new one to add to the list of people who've tried to do me in.

The action eventually died down and we boarded the boat home. It'd been a proper mental day out but a good one nonetheless. I'd made some money, got in the game for free and had a row with some Paddies: what more could I have asked for, apart from maybe someone chucking the Scousers overboard?

Although my allegiance lies with United rather than with England, it's always good to take a trip to another country with the lads. It provided some quality memories and it beat sitting about in Gorton any day.

Galley's overseas adventure demonstrates how easily trouble can find you when you go abroad to watch the football. In our case trouble is usually the purpose of our trip, so it's a plus point if the locals take exception to us being there. The bigger the chance of confrontation, the more made-up United are.

Although we welcomed brawls wherever we were playing, there was still one mob we were rightfully scared of. They were the biggest firm going and weren't afraid to get their hands dirty to take our lads down: the Greater Manchester Police, the only lads that could put United off going to a game. Other crews placed limits on the lengths to which they were willing to go to in order to get a result over us, but those boys were determined to take us out of the frame by any means necessary.

The early 90s marked a change in the way the Old Bill dealt with hooligans. They had previously only been concerned with nicking us on a match day, but then they started devoting every waking moment to trying to snare us – and in November 1990, they came very close indeed.

20
United Get Busted

The first sign that trouble was brewing came when one of our older pickpockets warned us the Old Bill were giving off a funny vibe.

'You lads need to calm down and take it easy for a while,' he told us one day while we were chilling with him in Ardwick Green. 'There's a raid coming; I can feel it. Haven't you seen the way those cunts in blue have been acting? There's definitely something going on.'

'We'll be okay,' I assured him. 'We can handle ourselves.'

To be honest, none of the boys really paid him any mind. We were young, hot-headed and didn't listen to anyone. It wasn't until we witnessed the police's shady behaviour firsthand that we decided to tone things down a bit. They started pulling well-known faces at the games and getting their details, which was suspicious because we knew they were already fully aware of who these lads were.

The problem was that we didn't always need to go out looking for a row in order to get one. Sometimes other mobs would bring it to us and we would be forced to defend ourselves. This meant that we still got our fair share of action even though we were trying to keep a low profile. We should have stayed away altogether though, because on November 22, the cops came hammering on my door. They had smug grins on their faces, as if they had been waiting for this moment for ages.

'We're arresting you on suspicion of involvement in a number of violent incidents at football over the course of the last

15 months. You don't have to say anything but anything that you do say can and will be used in evidence against you.'

It turned out that they had been doing surveillance on the Grey Parrot in Hulme, which was one of our main boozers. They had sat in cars outside the pub, filming us and gathering evidence. There had also been surveillance at some of the away games and the Old Bill were convinced they had enough footage to take the firm's main players off the scene.

Twenty-six lads were swooped upon that day at addresses in Manchester, London, Leeds, Barnsley and Bedford. Each suspect was taken to a different nick in the Northwest so that they couldn't corroborate their stories in the cells. The Cockney Reds were driven all the way to Manchester from London, which must have pissed them off no end.

One of the Cockneys was a university lecturer and got dragged out of the classroom during a lesson. None of us had known what he did for a living up until this point, so it came as a bit of a shock when we were told. He never talked about his work but we'd all assumed this was because he did something illegal. I suppose he must have needed to relieve stress on a match day after a week of marking essays.

The coppers took me to Salford Crescent police station, asked me a couple of questions and then remanded me to the detention centre above Manchester Magistrates' Court, where the rest of our firm had already been banged up. The other inmates seemed impressed that we were in there for defending the honour of the local team and plied us with Mars Bars, which were a luxury in jail. It was nice to know we were appreciated by some of the city's residents, even if Greater Manchester Old Bill were trying to have us locked away until we were old enough to collect our pensions. They'd ploughed so much money into the operation that they didn't want us back on the terraces until people were flying around on hover boards and shooting each other with laser guns.

The following day we were cuffed up and taken down to court, much to the disgust of Judge Owen, who was presiding over the case.

'Take those handcuffs off these men,' he ordered the guards. 'You're treating them like animals.' I'd heard about Owen before. He was supposed to be a strict cunt but very fair.

'You are all to be granted bail,' he told us once our cuffs had been removed. 'Your conditions are as follows: you are to remain at your addresses between the hours of 8am and 8pm, you are required to report to the nearest police station at 3pm every Saturday, you are not to attend any football matches and you are banned from all licensed premises in Manchester, Salford and Trafford until the day of your trial.'

This meant we couldn't even go in an off licence. They were a harsh set of conditions but at least we'd been granted a spell of temporary freedom. As I left the court, I felt relieved but at the same time overwhelmed by the struggle I now faced. My brief was going to need his wits about him at the hearing. The coppers had really gone to town on us and seemed determined to deprive us of our freedom.

As the weeks went by, being banned from the boozer started to get to me. The pub was like a second home to me; it was where I spent most of my time. Being on bail was a major ball-ache. I couldn't wait until my trial date to know whether I'd either go to jail and get my sentence over with or get a 'not guilty' and carry on with my life.

The rest of the mob found it just as difficult to keep to their bail conditions. Robert fucked them off and went to the boozer anyway, which nearly got him remanded. He was sitting drinking his pint one day when two undercover Old Bill approached him, wanting to know if he could get them any Es.

'Yeah, no problem,' Robert told them. 'Wait here while I get them.'

He was walking over to a dealer he knew to get some to sell on when the coppers ran across and grabbed him. 'Which one are you, Martin or Robert?' PC Plod asked him.

'Why, what are you nicking me for?' Robert asked, attempting to play it cool. He hadn't got any drugs on him so he knew they couldn't do him for possession or supply.

'You're banned from every licensed premises,' the officer told him. 'You shouldn't be in here.'

This was bad news. If he got his bail revoked then he could end up doing a fair whack behind bars as it was looking to be a long, drawn-out case.

'I'm Robert,' he conceded. 'Go on, read me my rights then.'

The Dibble took him down to the station and arraigned him to court to see if his breach was worthy of jail. Fortunately, the judge decided it wasn't, which saved him from being banged up until the day of the hearing. He'd had a narrow escape, although there are far worse things you can do while awaiting trial – for example, bubbling to the Five-O, which is what our mate Fat Andy did. It was Andy's first experience with the police – he shat himself and turned bandit on us. Luckily for him, none of the lads held it against him. We weren't particularly made-up but it was just one of those things.

By the time we were finally due in court, I was itching to put an end to the uncertainty. I didn't fancy the idea of doing a long stint in the slammer, but knew I'd have to take whatever I was given.

'I would like to request permission for the undercover officers involved in this case to provide their statements from behind a screen in order to protect their identities,' the copper in charge of the operation told Judge Owen once we were all seated.

United Get Busted

Owen wasn't having any of it. 'Unfortunately, I cannot allow that to happen in my court,' he said. 'It is important for the defendants to know who is testifying against them.'

'Some of the officers are involved in criminal investigations that involve men in the court today so they need to remain anonymous,' the Dibble tried to persuade him. 'It is of utmost importance for their safety. If it isn't possible to have a screen, would they be permitted to wear balaclavas over their faces?'

'No, they most certainly would not,' Owen shot him down. 'I will not have policemen dressed as IRA terrorists in my courtroom.'

I smiled at Robert, as if to say, 'They've fucked it now.' The copper went on to give a lengthy monologue about how dangerous we were and how badly we needed to be locked away. He used military terminology to refer to the role each lad played in the mob, labelling us 'captains', 'lieutenants' and 'armourers', which we thought was a bit over the top. I don't know how he could claim somebody gathering bricks and bottles to lob at a rival mob was an 'armourer' while keeping a straight face. Owen didn't seem particularly amused.

'Not even the police are safe from them,' the officer carried on, seemingly oblivious to the effect he was having upon the judge. 'At the start of the operation, two members of the force were assaulted during the course of their investigations.'

'In that case, why have you taken so long to bring the perpetrator of this attack to justice?' Owen asked him.

The copper was stumped. He had no idea how to respond and spent the next five minutes humming and hawing. The case was eventually thrown out but the police had spent so much on it that they appealed to the High Court, and then to the House of Lords, in an attempt to get it reinstated. It took three long years for the confirmation to come through that it wasn't going to proceed, which seemed like an eternity with bail conditions as strict as ours.

It was 1993 by the time we knew for certain we'd been let off the hook. The court sent us letters to inform us that the charges against us were no longer being pursued, which enabled me to breathe a huge sigh of relief. I was straight on the blower to the boys to organise a celebratory piss-up. We spent the next 24 hours getting off our faces, laughing and joking about what a shambles the Old Bill had made of everything. They'd wasted a year and three months putting together a case with more holes in it than Daniella Westbrook's nose.

Although nobody was jailed as a result of their efforts, the police still achieved a degree of success in damaging our firm. We knew it would be impossible to carry on causing havoc now we had so much heat on us. By this stage I had kids and could no longer risk being sent down, so I decided it was a good time to call it a day. I stopped fighting at the footy, packed in the thieving and focused my attention on the rave scene instead. The threat of prison had scared me straight, which was something I thought could never happen.

A lot of other lads went the same way as me. It was obvious that the Old Bill were going to come down on us like a ton of bricks the next time we stepped out of line, so some of the more established thugs hung up their gloves, making way for new faces to gain a foothold in the mob. A crew of younger lads from Moston came up through the ranks to fill the void and lads from Hibs' Capital Service Crew started tagging along, which was the catalyst for the next major chapter in United's history.

Our friends from north of the border had cottoned onto the fact they were less likely to be identified on CCTV footage if they all dressed in dark clothing and soon influenced our firm to do the same. Before we knew it, the media had labelled a section of our mob as the 'Men in Black' and black Sprayways and North Face jackets had replaced the Madchester influence that dominated the terraces in the early 90s. United now had their own uniform to go to battle in.

The MIB contained a mixture of seasoned veterans and fresh-faced up-and-comers. Although I was never part of this crew, they were United's top lads at the time so I've included a chapter based on what I've been told by those in the know. They are one of the Red Devils' best-known firms, so I could hardly write a book about our hooligans and exclude them.

21
The Men in Black

Men in Black was never a name to be taken seriously; it was a bit of a piss-take. United always shunned 'official' handles for our mob. Cheesy nicknames seemed a bit childish so we just referred to ourselves as the Reds. The press, on the other hand, have called us many things over the years – including the Inter City Jibbers and the Young Munichs, even though these names were never seen as anything more than just a joke, so you can imagine how made-up they were when the whole MIB thing came about. As far as the press were concerned, the boys now had a name reflecting a degree of organisation within the mob. The fact that the MIB all dressed the same supposedly proved that their violence was premeditated rather than spontaneous; it gave the impression they were better coordinated than your average football firm.

The lads mainly wore black for practical purposes. It meant they could easily identify who was on their side and made them harder to pick out on video footage. I'd be lying if I told you that there wasn't an element of intimidation to it as well, because the sight of a few hundred blacked-up figures walking down the street was enough to give even the most hardened rivals a bad case of the trots. The dress code added to the mystique surrounding the firm and kept local journalists busy as they wrote endless scare stories about this threat to the fabric of society.

The MIB caused chaos up and down the country. As time went on, the police raids became a distant memory and more and more lads joined the mob. It soon had a good 500 thugs, which made it Britain's biggest hooligan gang. Not only did United terrorise every team they came up against in Britain, they also started going abroad a lot more as we played a good number of European matches throughout the 90s. These trips overseas would usually result in clashes with the locals, who took exception to their town being overrun by thieves and hooligans.

Some countries' fans would fall back the minute our lads stood up to them but others were determined to shed some English blood. This was the case when the lads went over to see United play Galatasaray in the 1993 European Champions League. The Red Devils fans were totally oblivious to the danger that awaited them when they booked their flights to Istanbul. One hundred and sixty-four of our supporters arranged to go over on a flight arranged by a company called Millwest and another 30 bought seats on a chartered plane. We had drawn the Manchester leg of the game 3-3 so it looked set to be a proper exciting game.

The first signs of trouble came at the airport in Turkey, when the boys were greeted by a variety of different banners telling them they had just entered Hell. It wasn't the Turks that kicked the real mayhem off that day though; one of the MIB copped for £3000 worth of Turkish currency from behind the desk at the hotel reception, which caused the staff to go mad.

During the chaos, a lad from Salford decided it would be a good idea to hang an Israeli flag out of the window to wind the locals up. The minute the Turks caught sight of it, all hell broke loose. Bricks and stones came flying through the glass and our boys could only stand and stare as Turkish coppers bombarded the hotel with debris. People think that our Old Bill are bad, but they've got nothing on the Turks. Those cunts didn't give a fuck about the law; they were out purely for revenge.

The Men in Black

When they had eventually calmed down, the Dibble tried to blame the damage to the windows on the United lads. Some of our boys got banged up in Sagmalcilar prison, which is the nick featured in *Midnight Express*. God only knows what horrors they witnessed in there. I dare say it made the jails over here seem like luxury hotels.

The game itself was just as marred by corruption as the build-up to it had been. The Turkish coppers laid into Schemichel and Cantona as they left the pitch in full view of the TV cameras. The fact that the Old Bill were willing to leather our players in front of crowds of people shows how brazen they are over there. The police in Istanbul are animals.

In the aftermath of the game, the international press were quick to blame the fracas at the hotel on our hooligans: 'About 170 British soccer fans were arrested today after a disturbance at an Istanbul, Turkey, hotel before Manchester United was eliminated by Galatasaray of Istanbul in the European Champions Cup,' wrote a reporter for the *Seattle Times*. 'About 30 of the fans escaped from police custody. Seven were taken to court and another 140 awaited deportation. Staff at the Tamsa Hotel in the Aksaray district said fans wrecked 30 rooms, ransacked the lobby and stole money from a safe before the scoreless tie.'

The funny thing was that three of the supposed vandals were actually blind. What were they supposed to have done, gone on the rampage with their guide dogs and white sticks? Luckily, our MPs smelled a rat and put pressure on the Turks to carry out further investigations. The Turkish authorities soon realised that the windows had been smashed from outside and let all of the English suspects out of jail.

The boys were dicing with death by going to a country like that because a lot of people fail to make it out of Turkish prisons alive. It wasn't the only time they got in trouble overseas

HOTSHOT

either. Whenever United play in Europe, there are always a fair few arrests; some are for violence, others are for grafting. Some might think it foolish to go thieving in a country like Turkey but the MIB would never miss an opportunity to make a raise, no matter where they were.

The real moneymaking was done in the wealthier nations closer to home though. It makes a lot more sense to graft a place where money flows like water than it does to graft a place where nobody has a penny to their name. Some of the more business-minded lads got into doing hotels over in Belgium during this period. Galley was one such lad:

GALLEY

United's European games had a dual purpose for us: we loved to see how our team fared against clubs overseas, but also loved making money and couldn't pass up the opportunity to fill our pockets on the mainland. One way of doing this was to have a safe from a hotel. Sometimes our voyages abroad would go without a hitch, but every now and then something would go seriously wrong. By far our most infuriating grafting expedition was our journey to the Continent to see United play Dortmund. Martin copped for five grand from a bed and breakfast near Ostend on the way and it looked as if everything was going smoothly, until Eddie Beef started giving it the big 'un on the train. He was being a gobby bastard even though I'd paid his ferry over from England, so I told him to shut his fucking mouth, which he didn't take kindly to.

'Oh, so you want to know then, Gallagher, do you?' Eddie fronted me.

'Fucking right I want to know!' I told him. 'Get in the foyer right now and we'll have it.'

We were just gearing up to slug it out when the train stopped at Ghent and two Belgian Old Bill got on. They arrested me and Mar-

The Men in Black

tin for not having any tickets, leaving Eddie where he was – which was a bit annoying as he was the one who started it. Fortunately, being the quick thinker that he was, Martin managed to dump the money we'd stolen in a bin outside the Belgian Railway Police office as we were marched inside for questioning. This meant the Old Bill had nothing on us. They seemed more concerned about getting rid of us than pressing charges anyway. An officer briefly interviewed us and then escorted us onto a train to Ostend, where the ferries to England went from.

'Get the next boat back home and we will take no further action,' he told us once we'd reached our destination.

We acted as if we were going to obey his orders and then hopped onto a train to Ghent when the coast was clear, so that we could retrieve the cash from the bin. Neither of us had any other money so we were going to need it for the match. It was exactly where we'd left it, so I quickly picked it up and we hurried onto another rattler before the boys in blue got onto us.

We eventually managed to get to Germany, no thanks to Eddie. The problem was that by this stage our heads were proper burnt out and we had no idea which train we had to take to get to Dortmund. We ended up getting on the wrong one and going to some random town we had never heard of, which was a fucking nightmare considering how tired and fed up I was. To make matters worse, I spotted a familiar face milling around the platform, looking just as lost as Martin and me.

'It's fucking Eddie Beef,' I said to Martin. 'What the fuck is that cunt doing here?'

''Ey, less of that,' said Eddie. 'I'm dying for a bite to eat. Buy us a chicken sandwich will you, Gallagher?'

I couldn't help but smile even though he'd ruined the trip for us. It's difficult to stay mad at Eddie for too long because he's such a character.

'Let's just fuck the match off and go home,' I told him. 'You've *caused us no end of bother, you know that, don't you?'*

Eddie grinned sheepishly, as if to say, 'Yeah, I know, but you should still get me the sandwich.'

He wasn't in the least fazed by the fact he'd almost cost us five grand and our freedom; all he could think about was getting some scran. That's Eddie for you; he's a top-class jibber but a bit of a wild card. You can always count on him to add an element of unpredictability to a routine grafting trip.

Another United lad called 'B' had a similar experience with him in the late 90s. B had borrowed my passport to travel to France on, even though he looked fuck-all like me. He should have been attempting to keep a low profile so that the Hector didn't get onto it, but he made the mistake of taking Beef along. Partway through the trip, Eddie spotted a passenger sleeping with his mouth wide open and couldn't resist drawing a beard and glasses on the poor cunt with a can of shaving foam.

The fella still didn't wake up, so Eddie took things up a notch and sprayed foam in his mouth. This time Sleeping Beauty finally awoke and didn't seem best pleased. After calling B and Eddie every name under the sun, he eventually grassed them up to the Old Bill. B had my passport on him and had no choice but to tear it up in his pocket so they wouldn't get onto it. Which I suppose was my own fault for agreeing to lend it to somebody who looked as similar to me as Michelle McManus does to Cheryl Cole. He ended up getting released without charge so, from his perspective, things worked out for the best. One thing is for certain though: he would have had a much more trouble-free journey if it wasn't for Eddie Beef. Eddie has got a proper mischievous streak to him and can never resist causing chaos wherever he goes.

The Men in Black

While Eddie was keeping the Old Bill on their toes on the Continent, the rest of the Red Army were giving the Dibble over here an equally hard time. The Salford lot had started following Mancunian boxer Steve 'The Viking' Foster, which raised fears about hooliganism rearing its head in the boxing world. Steve's fans weren't the only 'boxing hooligans' to emerge during this period either; the Zulus had taken to supporting Brummie combatant Robert McCracken, which led to a full-scale riot when the two pugilists fought each other in September '94.

It wasn't just football lads who turned out to watch Steve that day; half of Salford travelled down to Birmingham for their local hero. The Viking was especially popular amongst the criminal fraternity and drew his fair share of villains. Ram raiders, gangsters and local hard men all came together to form the ultimate fighting team.

I wasn't there to witness the row firsthand but the footage is up on YouTube for all to see. Chairs were hurled back and forth across the NEC Arena and the two firms gave it to each other proper.

'The problems arose because rival sets of fans, fuelled by drink, were able to get at each other,' wrote Nick Halling of *The Independent* in the aftermath of the brawl. 'The real losers are the likes of McCracken and Foster, genuine men who are being undermined by a small percentage of idiots ... The thugs who have attached themselves to him are endangering a promising career.'

The incident prompted calls for a ban on alcohol during boxing matches and caused the NEC Security a whole heap of grief. It also demonstrated to the world that we were prepared to have a ruck at sporting events completely unrelated to football. It was another feather in United's cap and cemented our reputation as the firm that would riot anytime, anyplace, anywhere.

HOTSHOT

You're probably wondering what I was doing while all this was going on. Those of you who've been involved in football violence will know how difficult it is to stay away and no doubt consider it a miracle that I didn't come out of retirement. With United ransacking the Continent and teaming up with Salford's finest to have it out at the boxing, it would have been easy for me to lapse back into my old ways if I hadn't had the party scene to move onto. Causing damage to rival firms' faces was replaced by causing damage to my liver; the type of beats I delivered on the terraces were replaced by the type you could dance and take Es to. Rather than getting dressed up to have a fight, I'd get dressed up for a night on the piss. I was no longer Hotshot the Red Army hooligan; I was now Hotshot the 24-hour party head.

22
Twenty-Four Hour Party Thugs

Manchester was the place to be during the 90s. The drugs were good, the clubs were banging and there was an exciting vibe to the city, as if it was the centre of everything. Although it could never replicate the buzz of the terraces, going out and getting wrecked at its many rocking nightspots was a close second. I even had my own little party firm, which gave me the sense of camaraderie I'd had at the football. It was the perfect substitute

One of our favourite venues to get horribly off our faces at was a place called Taste in Hulme. It was a little café with a room upstairs that played house music. Most of the people who went there were quite shady but everybody knew each other, so it rarely went off. Epping Walk in Hulme was another regular haunt. There was a blues at a flat there that played acid house. God knows what the neighbours must have thought when they saw a load of pilled-up party people going in and out at stupid o'clock in the morning. They can't have been too pleased about it but what could they really do?

A club called Conspiracy in the city centre could be just as good, although it was a bit moody. There were always grafting firms from various different areas of Manchester knocking about. Nothing ever went off though because everyone was E'd up.

We never looked for trouble during our nights out, but it sometimes found us. A couple of the lads would try to make a bit of money from other partygoers, which occasionally resulted in violence. Then there were the football firms. It didn't matter to them that we were no longer active; if they saw us at a club then we were having it.

One of the most memorable clashes we had with a footy mob on a night out happened at a club called Maxime's in Wigan town centre. We were having a piss-up there with a couple of our City mates when a group of Liverpool lads showed up to cause some shit. A cocky-looking Scouser bowled straight over to my pal Little Brooksy and cracked him in the eye, which caused a doorman to beckon Brooksy over to see what was going on.

'What's happened to your eye?' the fella asked.

Brooksy had a shiner-and-a-half, but managed to convince the bouncer he'd come in with it. Those Scouse twats had nearly got us chucked out. They were going to pay for throwing their weight around like that.

Sure enough, when we eventually left the club the Liverpool lads were there, waiting to have a go. It kicked off big-time and one of them slashed me down the side of the leg with a broken bottle. I thought I'd been stabbed at first; blood was pouring out and there were shards of glass stuck in the cut.

We had a quick toe to toe with the Mickeys and soon got them on their toes. None of us had gone out looking for a fight; we went to have a drink and a dance and ended up leathering a group of Scousers, which was even better. We were all unarmed and a few of our opponents were tooled up, so it was a major result.

Our party firm might occasionally have got caught up in rucks, but violence was usually the last thing on our minds during a piss-up. We preferred a peaceful, hassle-free night out where we drank too much and took so many drugs that we could barely raise our fists. We didn't need a row to spice up our partying sessions because they were extreme enough as it was.

Twenty-Four Hour Party Thugs

One of our maddest benders lasted a whole three months. We caught a bit of shuteye here and there but didn't have a sober minute. A lot of crazy things happened during the time that we were out of it. We were at the Dry Bar on Oldham Street when, for whatever reason, I decided to climb up on the windscreen of somebody's car. The next thing I knew, I was being driven around the city centre at top speed and everybody else was pissing themselves with laughter. Every time the car went round a corner, I yelled, 'Stop the fucking car!' which the boys all cracked up at.

The highlight of the bender was our appearance in a Black Grape video. I was drinking at the Dry Bar with the lads when Bez came in and asked us if we would be up for dancing about in the background.

'You'll get paid £50 each,' he said. 'We're filming it in Ancoats later today.'

I'd known Bez for a while because he was a friend of a United lad called Long Legs. We didn't even see him as being famous, we just saw him as one of the boys. Black Grape were scallies like us so we could relate to them, which is probably why we liked their music so much. It was raw and working class, without any pretensions.

'Count us in,' I said, looking forward to my 15 minutes of fame.

It's not every day you get a cameo in a video for a song by one of your favourite groups. I was high on everything under the sun, so dancing enthusiastically would be no problem whatsoever.

We spent the day filming in Ancoats then went on to a city-centre bar called Home. I was chilling out on the balcony, sniffing poppers and talking about the vid, when the next thing I knew I'd lost my balance and fallen 15 feet onto the floor. Luckily, my body was so relaxed from drink and drugs that I was perfectly okay. The bouncers weren't too happy about it though, and told us all to leave.

A couple of months later, all of the boys were crowded round the TV, waiting for the first showing of the video on *Top of the Pops*. Everybody was hoping that the camera would pan in on them, but the only lads you could see were me, Brooksy and Eddie Beef. There was a one-second clip of us dancing, which was just long enough to make out who we were. It was a buzz seeing ourselves on TV, but I don't think I'll have Hollywood directors calling at my door anytime this century.

A 2003 issue of the fanzine *United We Stand* brought up my appearance in the video and described some of my adventures following the Reds: 'Hotshot made a cameo appearance in the 1995 Black Grape video "The Reverend Black Grape". As band member Kermit sings the line, "Can I get a witness?" the camera pans on to a watching crowd. If you're quick with the pause button you can just make out the top of his head at the front. This stunning video debut has unsurprisingly not led to any further acting roles for Hotshot.'

Although it could never quite fully replace the excitement of my fighting years, partying gave me something to do after the police had sucked all the fun out of the footy. If I hadn't had beer, coke, Es, trips and countless other substances then I don't know what else I would have done. I probably wouldn't have so many gaps in my memory but I'd have missed out on some top-notch adventures.

23
Prankchester United

My party years were also the period when I got to know Karl 'Fat Neck' Power, who is famous for pulling hilarious pranks at sporting events. He has blagged his way onto Centre Court at Wimbledon, posed as an England rugby international in Rome and even appeared in a United team photo. Internet search engine Yahoo included him in their list of greatest ever pitch invaders and *The Guardian* have hailed him as 'Britain's greatest interloper'.

Fat Neck first caught the attention of the media in April 2001, when he walked onto the pitch in team colours before a Champion's League game against Bayern Munich. Some of the players cottoned onto him but nobody blew his cover. He has since been the focus of a Channel 4 documentary and had a Black Grape song named after him. To me though, he will always be 'the whistling man from Ancoats'.

I called Fat Neck 'the whistling man' because he always whistled to get my attention when he called round at my house. He was a first-class party animal and we'd go on wild drinking sessions together. It was during one of these nights out that he told me about his plan to get a bunch of lads together to pretend to be players at Old Trafford and scam their way onto the pitch. It was a similar prank to his 2001 stunt but on a larger scale. Another infamous prankster called Tommy Dunn was onboard for it, but a couple more people were still needed to complete the squad.

'I'm well up for that,' I said, thinking what a rush it would be to set foot on that hallowed turf. 'You can count me in.'

HOTSHOT

The plan was to re-enact Jerzy Dudek's blunder against United at Anfield in December 2002, when he let a header through his legs, leaving Diego Forlan to tap the ball into the net. We were playing Liverpool and it was bound to get a rise out of the Mickeys.

On the day of the stunt, I was so excited that I felt like I'd taken a pill. I had written to *Jim'll Fix* It as a young 'un, asking him to get me on the pitch at Old Trafford, but he never got back to me. It was probably a fucking good thing as well, given the recent revelations about him.

So I was lucky I had Fat Neck to make my childhood dream come true. As we jibbed our way into the ground, my whole body tingled with anticipation. This was it: the moment of reckoning. We managed to blag our way into the tunnel but then my heart sank as I saw a locked gate at the end, blocking us from our destiny.

'What are you lads here for?' asked a member of staff, looking as if he was trying to work out who the hell we were.

'We're the pre-match sponsorship group,' Fat Neck blagged him. 'Quick, let us out!'

The fella bought our story and took the key out of his pocket. As it turned in the lock, I felt on top of the world. I was going to do something many people would give their right arm for: I was walking out onto Old Trafford in full United kit.

Words can't begin to describe the buzz I got from running out through that gate. It was better than any drug I've ever taken and believe me, I've taken a lot. We adopted the team pose in the centre circle then ran over to Liverpool's end and performed the stunt to rapturous applause. The Scousers were fuming; so much for their famous sense of humour.

For some bizarre reason, the Old Bill waited until we'd finished the prank before they arrested us. They left it until we got outside the ground, then cuffed us up and took us to Stretford police station, where we were charged with using disorderly or threatening behaviour and illegally entering a football pitch. I ended up getting a three-year ban and being barred from every stadium in Europe, but it was worth it for an experience like that. I would have willingly taken any punishment I was given.

Here's what *United We Stand* had to say in the aftermath of the prank:

Name: ?
Aliases: Hotshot, Hotpot, H, Jimmy Krankie.
Age: 32.
Lives: Sunny Gorton.
Sits: Anywhere I can jib in.
First game: Coventry at home 1980.
Best game: European Cup Final 1999.
Favourite ever player: Bryan Robson.
Favourite current player: Roy Keane.
Worst moment as a Red: Getting beat 5-1 off The Shit in '89. I was on my way home eating me chips and gravy when some Dibble pulled up next to me in their van, got hold of the tray and poured it all down me coat. They then drove off all laughing their bollocks off. I felt pretty low at that point.
Best moment as a Red: It's got to be Barcelona. It doesn't get any better than that. I got knocked back with two snides so I decided to just leg it past the Spanish Dibble. They caught me though. So I kept doing it again and again, getting thrown out then just legging it when I got back to the turnstile. In the end, I think they got fed up of chasing me and just let us in.

HOTSHOT

Most despised opposition: City.
All time United 11: Schmeichel, Irwin, McGrath, Bruce, Albiston, Milne, Keane, Robson, Giggs, Cantona, Van Nistlerooy.

Minutes before United took to the field in their 4–0 demolition of Liverpool at the end of last season, Hotshot, along with Karl Power and nine others, were busy jibbing their way through the turnstiles, past stewards and security guards. They were wearing full United kits in order to commemorate Jerzy Dudek's timeless fuckup in the corresponding fixture at Anfield last season. A five foot one colossus and being just the better side of being bald, Hotshot was the obvious choice to be the group's Barthez.

The group practised the stunt on an Astroturf in Newton Heath and perfected it to last just over a minute. The actual stunt took a little longer following extended celebrations in front of the travelling Liverpool support. The stunt was greeted by bemused laughter from United fans as they went from team pose in the centre circle to recreate Diego's finest moment and then on to celebrate in front of the visiting fans. Hotshot describes being on the Old Trafford pitch as a 'proper buzz'. It was apparent from the off that this was simply a prank in which the only victims were the red-faced Old Trafford security staff who were well and truly caught with their pants down.

However, all 11 were arrested and charged with using disorderly or threatening behaviour (Public Order Act 1986) and entering the field of play without sufficient reason (Football Act 1991). They look to be getting three-year bans at least, a punishment usually only given in hooliganism cases. This would be especially harsh as all of the lads are big Reds who happened to realise that most common of schoolboy dreams by running out in full kit to a packed Old Trafford and leaving to a standing ovation. Even Alan Brazil can't claim that.

Fuel was then poured onto the fire as five Liverpool fans came forward as witnesses for the prosecution claiming angry scenes in the visitors section that day, sparked off by the mock celebrations. Maybe it was the fact that Karl Power was wearing a 'Les Battersby is innocent' t-shirt that really got their blood boiling. Or was it that Tommy Dunn, the brains behind the scam, was sporting a ridiculous Forlan-style wig? So much for that famed Scouse sense of humour.

It eventually took four police officers and two horses to arrest Hotshot as he and his teammates tried to make their escape across the Old Trafford forecourt following their on-field antics. They are back in court on the 8 December.

The media had a field day over our antics. 'SERIAL prankster Karl Power has stunned Manchester United chiefs AGAIN after leading out a joke version of the team at Old Trafford,' wrote *The Sun*. 'Karl, 33, famous for posing with the Red Devils at a Champions League match in Munich, gave thousands of amazed fans another giggle with his biggest stunt yet.'

The police were less amused and tried to claim we'd jeopardised the safety of the fans. 'Their actions have been greeted with disdain at Old Trafford, with serious concerns being raised over security arrangements at the ground, which will stage this season's Champions League final at the end of next month,' they told the paper.

Personally I thought it was hilarious. The Dibble were just pissed off because the public were left wondering why the officers at the stadium had let it happen. Nobody was hurt and the nation had a laugh at the expense of the Scousers. Where's the crime in that, I ask you?

24
Trouble Overseas

One of the reasons the Old Bill came down so hard on us for the prank may have been that they were still struggling to keep a lid on violence at the football. From their perspective, invading the pitch to take the piss out of the Mickeys was only a gnat's whisker away from invading it to kick off. By this stage the action had moved away from the stadium and usually went on in more discreet locations, but to say that the police had eradicated the 'English disease' completely would be to deny reality.

While those clueless scabs were busy nicking people for playing harmless practical jokes, the MIB were mobbing up and rioting. The 2000s saw the criminal side of the firm dying down a bit and brawling once again taking priority. United were feared less for their gangster connections than for handiness with their fists.

The Red Devils continued to do well on the pitch, dominating the league and making several successful ventures into Europe. The difference between the noughties and the previous decades was that teams from the mainland were now just as up for it as the Brits. Films like *Green Street* and *The Football Factory* had turned the world onto organised football violence. Polish and Russian mobs went from strength to strength and fans all over the world started wearing casual clothing and calling themselves 'lads'.

Foreign mobs also started bringing it to our manor. In previous decades it would have been unheard of for a team from overseas to show up with a firm in Manny, but the turn of the millennium saw them getting their act together. It wasn't just copycat casuals either: the Italians had their own unique brand of violent fans, known as 'Ultras'. They'd existed since the late 60s and developed independently of our homegrown thugs. Galley had a run-in with them when we played Roma in the mid 2000s:

GALLEY

The first sign of trouble came when a lad called 'G' turned up at the boozer covered in blood, with a huge gash down his back.

'Fucking hell, what happened to you?' I asked him. 'You look like you've had a back rub from Edward Scissorhands.'

'It's those fucking Eyeties,' he told me. Watch it Galley; they're ripping the top off coke cans, folding the metal around to make blades and chivving people up with them. I've never seen anything like it.'

We've been known to use car aerials as whips and fashion the occasional 'Millwall brick' out of a newspaper, this being a type of makeshift baton that was popular during the 70s because it was easy to make and the Old Bill could hardly pull someone for having a paper on them.

But this was taking things to another level. I wanted to see it for myself so I headed out onto the streets and, sure enough, a mob of 200 tooled-up Ultras were going at it with our lads. The Eyeties were doing okay but I don't think they'd have been up to much if they didn't have their blades. They were all in top-notch Italian labels and seemed more interested in looking good than fighting.

There were running battles up and down Warwick Road for a good ten minutes before the police eventually managed to herd Roma towards the stadium. Some of them tried to get past the Old Bill to get at us, but they ended up getting slapped and running back behind the escort. They seemed as if they were the type of lads who were only brave when armed to the teeth. If none of them had been tooled up we'd have gone through them in minutes.

Roma were nothing special, weapons or no weapons. My lasting impression of Italian Ultras is that they belong on a catwalk, not at the football. It's fashion first, fists second with the Eyeties, which is the direct opposite to the way our lads see things. I like to look good on a match day but would have a row in rags if I'd nothing else available. Roma need to stick to modelling their clobber and leave the hooliganism to us Brits. Respect to them for turning out, but they'll need to do better than that the next time they face the mighty Red Army.

A lot of foreign firms tended to use knives, which isn't the way that battles should be fought. Personally I think blades make things more like armed combat than hooliganism. The turn of the millennium saw its fair share of tool-related tragedies overseas. Eddie witnessed one of the worst in Portugal. He might not have been in the least bit bothered about being locked up in a Thai prison, but this incident had a lasting impact on him which shows you how traumatic it was:

EDDIE

It was the 2004 European Championship and I'd managed to successfully jib my way over to watch England. The England fans were in high spirits, dancing the conga with St George's crosses painted across their faces, and there was no hint of malice in the air. Unfortunately, the good mood didn't last for long because an annoying-as-fuck Ukrainian bloke started pestering everyone for cigarettes and drinks. He was trying to pick people's pockets and kept coming back despite being told to fuck off.

HOTSHOT

Suddenly, without warning, the Ukrainian pulled out a blade and stabbed one of the England fans through the heart. His victim wasn't a hooligan; he was just your average run-of-the-mill shirter. Within minutes, the police were on the scene, dragging this crazed knifeman away. The kid that he had chivved was rushed to hospital, where he was pronounced dead on arrival.

We were all in a state of shock. The press didn't make things any easier; they offered money and pints to anybody who could give them details of the 'fight', which showed their intention to make out that the poor lad who was stabbed was a thug himself. I'm not a fan of the media at the best of times, but their behaviour that day was particularly disgusting. They attempted to brand an innocent murder victim as a hooligan, which was low even for them.

The killer was eventually sentenced to 13 years in prison, but his victim's family pointed out that he could be released in six for good behaviour. They told the papers they were devastated by the leniency of the punishment. The entire incident really hammered home how senseless violence at the football can be. Nobody expects to lose their life when they go to see a game. It was a sad, sad day and my heart goes out to the poor lad's friends and family.

It seems the tables have turned with regards to thieving as well as hooliganism. During my time on the scene it was the British who would pick foreign fans' pockets, rather than the other way around, but nowadays everybody wants to get in on the act. The difference between the Brits and the foreigners is that we would never randomly attack our targets if we didn't get what we were after. What happened in Portugal was a cowardly, indefensible act that cost an eager young England fan his life.

The other thing the Brits had to be on their guard against was being nicked for things they hadn't done. Because of our reputation as a nation of hooligans, the foreign Old Bill were quick to point the finger at our boys whenever there was a match on. This resulted in a lad called P-Macc being falsely accused of stabbing a German fan during the 2006 World Cup. It ruined his time over there and almost landed him with a lengthy stint behind bars. The media were just as eager to twist the story as they had been in Portugal. They printed a load of shite about how P had gone to the game tooled up, even though he was unarmed at the time of his arrest, and whipped a minor incident up into an attempt on someone's life.

P-Macc is one of a number of lads from Cheshire that United have had onboard throughout the years. He is somewhat atypical of the Reds in that he's always been a passionate follower of the England team. Although it's undeniable that he went across looking for trouble that day, his crime was blown completely out of proportion. Here's the man himself to tell you what went down:

P-MACC

I've always enjoyed watching England play away because it's exciting to get up to mischief in a foreign land. The minute I found out that the 2006 World Cup was being held in Germany, I made up my mind that I was going no matter what. I managed to get a cheap ticket to Amsterdam and spent a week doing bits and bobs until I earned enough to get to Frankfurt, where we were scheduled to play Paraguay in the group stages.

On the day of the match, I met up with some other English hooligans at a bar called O'Neill's and we jibbed into the ground. We won the game 1-0, with Paraguay's Carlos Gamarra scoring an own goal. The next match was in Nuremburg, so I hit the road again to see our team play Trinidad and Tobago. It was harder to jib into the stadium this time so I watched the game on a big screen in a fan festival park.

England won 2-0, with Peter Crouch scoring in the 83rd minute and Steven Gerrard scoring in the 90th.

The third England game was against Sweden in Cologne. As luck would have it, I saw the perfect opportunity for a graft before the match. I was in a restaurant with a load of other England fans when I noticed a wallet behind the counter. People were singing football songs and jumping around all over the place, which provided the perfect distraction while I snatched it. Within a split second I'd vaulted across the bar and jumped back over with the wallet. It contained 5,000 Euros, which is the equivalent of £4,300.

The wallet must have been used to store the restaurant's takings for the day. I shared the wealth around and sorted all of the other England fans out with some drinks. I then went out to buy myself some expensive clothes and booked into a posh four-star hotel.

England were playing their next game against Ecuador in Stuttgart, so I made my way to Heidelberg, which is relatively close. I spent two nights in a hotel with some lads from Torquay and then booked a room at a hotel in Stuttgart.

We decided to watch the match on a large television screen in a big square in the city centre. It was like the German equivalent to Manchester's Piccadilly Gardens. There were hundreds of other England fans in the square and they were singing 'Ten German Bombers' to wind the locals up, to the tune of 'Ten Green Bottles'. At around 5pm an Arabic-looking German guy came bouncing down the street, banging into people and trying his hardest to start some shit. He was obviously looking for some aggro, so I smacked him in the mouth and knocked the fucker's teeth out. The next thing I knew, 15 Old Bill had jumped on me. They shoved me in the back of a police van and started driving to the cop shop.

I was sitting in the sweatbox, wondering how the Dibble had got onto me so quickly, when I heard a voice from another section of the van say, 'Are you P from Macclesfield?' By sheer coincidence some lads that I'd met in Ibiza had been nicked just before I had.

Trouble Overseas

They'd been arrested for chucking plastic cups at a policeman.

I assumed that we'd be set free as soon as the game had finished, because none of us had committed a particularly serious offence. My assumption would probably have been accurate if the Arab hadn't lied and told the Old Bill that I'd stabbed him in the mouth. I'd knocked the fella's teeth out, which you can't do with a knife, so it was obvious to anybody with commonsense that he was hyping up his injuries to get a payout. You can leave a scar or a stab wound with a blade, but knocking someone's gnashers out takes a blow from something blunt.

I was eventually transported to a prison in Stuttgart and locked up in a dormitory with seven other English lads. There were boys from Leicester, Luton, Southampton, Nottingham, London and Moston in north Manchester, which was a godsend because I didn't fancy being the only English speaker in the nick. It was funny because the lad from Luton seemed the least suited to doing bird, despite the fact that he was a big, hard National Front supporter. He was crying his eyes out and going on about how he couldn't handle it inside. Fortunately, my other roommates had a little more emotional stability. The Notts lad was a major asset to our dorm because he was proper intimidating. He was a big, bald fella with a bit of weight on him, which made him look like a typical British bulldog. None of the other prisoners would start shit with him around.

There weren't actually that many Germans in the jail, strange as it might seem. I would say that only ten per cent of the other cons were Krauts; the rest of them were French, Turkish, English, Nigerian or Russian. There was a proper mix of different nationalities, which was good because it would have been weird as fuck if I was the only foreigner.

People say it's difficult in prison in the UK, but the regime here is nothing compared to what it's like in Stuttgart. We were banged up for 23 hours a day, including mealtimes. They brought the food up to our rooms, which was hardly worth it because the scran was fucking shite. We got a hard bread bun, a bit of cheese and some German tea without any milk or sugar. Our evening meal was delivered to the dorm at 4pm, which meant we had to starve all night. The system was designed to break the prisoners' resolve.

It would have been alright if I knew I would receive a short sentence, but the morning after I arrived there was a loud bang on the door and a German prison officer came striding into the dorm.

'You are bigger than Beckham,' he grinned.

What was this bloke on about?

'Bigger than Beckham,' he repeated, thrusting a newspaper under my nose to reveal my face on the front page.

'English hooligan expecting ten years for stabbing Iraqi,' read the caption above my photo.

This didn't bode well at all. The fact that the national press were on hand to take a picture was a little too convenient. It was as if they'd paid the Iraqi geezer to provoke me so that they could get a story.

The only redeeming feature of the jail was that it had a prison shop, which is a given over here but isn't always guaranteed in foreign nicks. I still had £100 worth of Euros left that I'd stolen from the restaurant, which enabled me to get by without having to rely on the meagre prison rations. It was a fucking good thing too because I'd have had a rotten time of it if I'd had to eat the rank shit they provided.

On 1 June, England were knocked out of the cup by Portugal and the other English prisoners were released one after another, presumably because they were no longer a threat. They had all paid decent lawyers to fight their cases, but a top-notch brief cost around 5,000 Euros which was more cash than I had. I wasn't about to ask my mum to send money across, as it was bad enough for her to find out I was in a German nick without me pestering her to pay my legal fees as well. This meant I was the last Englishman in the jail and had to knock about with a local lad who spoke a bit of English.

Trouble Overseas

'I'll tell you this now, P,' the lad told me one day during our time out of the cells. 'You couldn't have ended up in bigger shithole. This is the worst prison in Germany.'

I've since spoken to a couple of people who have grafted over there and they've told me the same. It was just my luck to get banged up in the roughest gaff in the land, although the worst was still to come because the prison guards had some news for me.

'Get your stuff, you're getting relocated,' said the head screw. 'We're putting you where we put all the shit.'

I was moved into a cell with seven Nigerians. Just before the move, one of the screws had asked me why my country was so full of Pakistanis. Putting me in with a load of Africans was probably his way of saying we were used to being surrounded by immigrants in England. The Nigerians spoke very broken English, which made it difficult to communicate. I had to sleep with one eye open because they seemed to stay awake all night as well. Most of them were in for fraud but some were in for people smuggling, and they definitely weren't the type of people I'd have associated with outside.

As well as constantly being on edge, I was also bored out of my skull because I couldn't have a decent conversation with my new cellmates. I even resorted to reading The Bible and finished the entire book twice over. Some of the other inmates entertained themselves by bullying other cons. A hefty Russian geezer seemed to think he could intimidate me into giving him my £800 watch. He was always asking me for it whenever I was out of the cell, so one day I decided to teach the cunt a lesson. The minute our door opened for exercise, I went and whacked the silly wanker. The next thing I knew, the entire landing had gone up and half the wing was stamping on my head. It was a case of 'get the Englishman'.

Shortly after the commotion had died down, one of the screws came over and told me I was getting moved. 'P,' he said, 'you're going to another wing. The inmate that you hit has got a lot of friends and you won't be safe here.'

HOTSHOT

That was all I needed; I'd gone and slapped the wing's Mr Big.

Fortunately, I didn't have to stay in the jail much longer because I was due in court in September. My court case couldn't have gone much better: it was revealed that a doctor had examined the Iraqi guy and concluded he'd been punched rather than stabbed. In light of this new evidence it was decided that I was to be released because I'd already spent four months inside.

On the way out of the jail, one of the screws bade me farewell and handed me a 50-gram tobacco pouch. You wouldn't get that from a British prison guard; they would just tell you to get on your way. I still had to get home though and had hardly any money. I'd have taken the discharge grant you get in England over the tobacco any day of the week.

I jibbed the train from Stuttgart to Frankfurt then got a train to Amsterdam, where I spent the next couple of nights relaxing and smoking weed. Once I'd finished sampling the delights of the 'Dam, I hopped aboard a £28 ferry from the Hook of Holland to Harwich and jibbed the train to Manchester. When I got back home, everybody was proper excited, telling me, 'You've been in the papers!' I really was 'bigger than Beckham'.

As the weeks went by, normality gradually returned. By December I was no longer the face of English hooliganism; I was P from Macclesfield, your average British citizen. Then there was a knock on the front door and the craziness started up again.

'Are you P?' It was the Old Bill. What the fuck had I done now?

'Yeah,' I told them. 'What the fuck have I done now?'

'We've been in touch with the German authorities and it's been decided that you've got to go to court in this country for the assault in Stuttgart.'

I'd already been tried and imprisoned in Germany. This was unbelievable. The judge at Macclesfield Magistrates issued me with a £600 fine and told me I had to hand my passport in at Long-sight police station whenever England played away or Man U played abroad. I still haven't paid the fine because I'd already served my time. How can you be punished for the same crime twice? It doesn't make any sense.

The result of the court case was featured in The Sun, the Manchester Evening News and the Macclesfield Express. It was proper embarrassing because everybody was whispering about me, saying that I'd let my country down.

Oh well. I'd had the holiday of a lifetime. It's just a shame that I spent four months of it inside and then had such a lousy welcome when I came home to Britain. The Old Bill are doubtless hoping that my German ordeal will put me off travelling abroad, but there's little chance of that. My overseas escapades have only just begun.

25
Same Shit, Different Era

What happened to P-Macc shows the lengths the Old Bill were willing to go to dissuade our thugs from sullying England's reputation overseas. The boys in blue were desperately attempting to undo the damage mobs like United had done to the country's image during the previous decades. They should really have been concentrating more upon what was going on over here, because there were still certain games where trouble was guaranteed.

The enmity between the Mancs and the Scousers was just as strong as ever; Bolton and Leeds still cursed the ground we walked upon. But by far the most action-packed games that United had were against Man City. A new generation had come onto the scene since the rave era had lessened the animosity between the two firms, and now the hatred for our City rivals was back at its peak again.

You would have thought City might have got their shit together by the turn of the millennium, but they were still no match for United. Every time they came up against the Reds our lads smashed them to bits. One of our most decisive victories over them took place in Ardwick towards the end of the decade. All of the lads who were there are adamant that they've never seen a mob get as badly pasted as The Shit did that day. Galley is one of them:

HOTSHOT

GALLEY

Derby day has always been a tense affair in Manchester. It's an occasion when the city is no longer a single entity; it becomes two separate hostile communities, one Red and one Blue. For some people this moody atmosphere manifests itself as a low, grumbling resentment, but for the Red Army there is no other option but to express it the only way we know how, which is by mobbing up and rioting.

This particular derby saw a group of 80 to 100 of United's finest gathering at a pub in Levenshulme, ready to get stuck into the Blues the minute we got word of their location. Sue enough, just as we were settling down to sup our pints the word went round that they'd plotted up at a nearby boozer. We were forced to quickly polish off our lagers and head out to have it with them.

As we approached the pub, we noticed a couple of Young Guvnors milling around outside so we got straight into them, kicking and punching like crazy. Much as it pains me to admit it, they were all proper up for it and put up a good fight. But we still overpowered them. The rest of the Blues came out to join the fray and, before we knew it, the streets had descended into a full-blown battleground. City's boozer was soon in tatters, with broken glass everywhere. Their lads were in a similar state and would have got it worse if the Old Bill hadn't turned up to put an end to it. None of us fancied missing the game on account of being locked up in the cells, so we all split up and went to different pubs.

Once the heat had finally died down, we got the mob back together and headed off into Ardwick, as there was a rumour that City had gone on to a watering hole in that neck of the woods. By the time we got to the boozer, they'd tooled themselves up with scaffolding poles from a nearby building site and looked as if they meant business. Iron bars or none, they were still going to get it. We'd already done them once that day and wasted no time in getting stuck back in.

City made the mistake of throwing their tools at us to try and keep us back, which was an idiotic move at best. We charged on through the hail of missiles and gave it to them bad-style. By the time we'd finished doing the business there were KO'd blue-conks strewn across the floor. I've never seen that many unconscious bodies after a fight in my life; it looked like something out of a Jackie Chan movie.

We didn't make it to the game in the end because we were too busy celebrating our victory. I daresay none of The Shit went to it either because 90 percent of them were smashed to fuck. That's not to say they didn't have a game set of lads with them – they all stood and fought, which is more than can be said for some teams' firms. They just couldn't compare to the Reds, which has been a running theme throughout every chapter of this book.

So there you go; Galley and the boys were still slapping City about the place over a decade after I'd left the scene. Although I no longer participated in the violence myself, I always kept my ear to the street and remained in the loop, enabling me to keep clued up on every victory over our bitter blue neighbours. There's nothing like a load of City getting their heads kicked in to put a smile on the face of an ex-Red Army thug.

26
Pev's Story

My retirement from the hooligan world also provided me with the opportunity to trade war stories with other old faces. Some of them were lads that I'd fought alongside; others were active before I threw my first punch at a match. Up until this point, I had only known about the experiences of lads I went to the games with, so it was nice to hear other people's perspectives on the pastime I once held such a passion for.

One of the more interesting characters I spoke to during this period was a fella known as Pev, a Salford hooligan from the 70s. He had been part of a subculture called the 'townies', who were the predecessors to the Perry boys. Pev was a fascinating character. He was very self-analytical and able to pinpoint the exact sequence of events that led him to become a thug. He also knew more about the origins of the link between fashion and hooliganism than anybody I'd ever spoken to. This vintage hooligan's story was so interesting that I've asked him to contribute a chapter. His experiences provide an insight into what was going on at Old Trafford before I came onto the scene – the fashion, fights and tunes that went on to influence the current Red Army:

PEV

I am contributing to this book in order to document a social movement. Hopefully, what I have written will not come across as self-serving, vainglorious or egotistical, because it is just an honest attempt to relay my experiences. Growing up, I didn't have the typical home life that people might associate with hooligans. My parents were strict Roman Catholics to the point where, earlier on in his life, my old man went to mass three times each Sunday: nine o'clock, ten o'clock and six o'clock. He was a firm believer in Jesus and a very conscientious person, as were the entire family. My uncles Harry and Bernard both helped out at Salford Lads Club, with Bernard even receiving a posthumous award for his work. We were a very moral and community-spirited lot.

Dad was extremely hard-working down the mines. He lost three of his toes in an accident while putting food on our table and spent a lot of time in a miners' convalescent home in Southport. This made things harder for my mam because we didn't have any money coming in during that period. The pits eventually closed down, which was an even worse turn of events. I could see the change in Dad the minute he lost his job. Mining was all that he'd known since age 14 and he was rightfully devastated.

Although I lived in a village on the edge of Salford, I spent a lot of time with my Uncle Harry in Ordsall. He owned a newsagents on Robert Hall Street, one down from Archie Street where they used to film Coronation Street. That should give you an idea of the type of place it was: your typical Mancunian terraced housing estate.

Ordsall had a reputation for being rough and ready, but I never got any grief there. Maybe it was because everybody wanted to stay on the good side of my family, so that my aunt and uncle would allow them to buy from the shop on credit. I used to help my Uncle Harry deliver the papers, which I always enjoyed. Sometimes I'd hear a massive roar that sounded like an earthquake and ask him what it was.

'That's Old Trafford,' he would say. 'That's where Georgie Best plays football.'

I remember thinking, Wow, I've got to go there one day.

As I got older, the government started pulling down the housing blocks as part of their slum clearance policy and the Salford I knew and loved began to disappear. Uncle Harry's shop was the last building to go because the demolition workers needed somewhere to buy *Park Drive fags*, *Swan Vestas matches* and the Manchester Evening News. *I was devastated to see the place I grew up in turning into a wasteland. It felt as if everything was changing.*

When I was in the third year of junior school, I began to think the government's desire to demolish the community and put families in high-rise flats summed up their overall attitude towards us. I realised that society was structured so that working-class kids could only get so far, which caused me to start acting up in school. I was still a smart kid though, so I sat the entrance exam for Salford's top grammar school, De Le Salle College, which was where Anthony 'Mr Manchester' Wilson had gone to.

I passed the exam with flying colours, but the teachers at my juniors wouldn't send me to De La Salle because they were concerned that a livewire like me might give them a bad reputation. 'We want you to go to a comprehensive instead,' I was told. 'You'll be top of the class if you go there.'

At the start of the first term at the comprehensive, we had to do a test to see who would be put in which class. I ended up coming about sixth or seventh out of the entire year and being placed in the top class. The few lads who were cleverer than me were mostly from West Leigh, which was quite a poor area. It was obvious that they should all have gone to a grammar school but had been deprived of a place because of their postcodes. This made me even more frustrated and I thought, what's the point of being here if it's going to be like this?

I always felt as if I was never given ways to channel my skills. Football was one of my main passions. I played for one of the best schoolboy teams in the Northwest but my school didn't even have a footy team. They seemed to be failing me in every possible area.

English was another subject I was good at. I used to love writing stories and poems. With that in mind, you can imagine how pissed off I was when I was handed back a poem that I'd done for my homework and told I'd copied it from a book. That was the last fucking straw! From that moment onwards I bunked off school as often as I could and disrupted every lesson I went to. The fact that I understood what was going on around me made me rebel against the system. That was one of the reasons I became a hooligan. My time with the Red Army was born out of frustration at the way society worked.

In '73, the Reds became my world. From that year onwards you couldn't keep me away from the games. I first decided that I wanted to be a hooligan at a midweek game in Norwich. I'd been going to home games with a few lads from Leigh, Atherton and Tyldesley, who I proudly stood with on the Stretford End, but this was something else. I met a young rabble whose arrogance and nerve hypnotised me. These boys had an aura of confidence that I'd never seen before.

I went on to cause no end of mischief with that very same group of lads. My friends and I would always sit on a set of steps near a shop called Chelsea Girl in town before the home games. This was our meeting point and could have been the reason we were later labelled 'townies'.

You could get to London for next to nothing when United were in the second division. All you had to do was pay 2p for the bus into town, walk to Oxford Road station, jib the train to Knutsford and then hitchhike to the capital from Knutsford service station. We'd figured out a way of getting into home games for free as well. Some of the lads worked out that you could sneak into the Scoreboard Paddock through the door marked 'Officials and Players Only' before the turnstiles opened. Then all you needed to do was hide in the toilets until you heard the clicking of the stiles. A commissioner stood on the door at 1.30 prompt so we made sure that we were in for 1.20.

When it came to jibbing into stadiums, our determination knew no boundaries. I remember a game against Derby County where I thought we were never going to get in. It was the semi-final of the FA Cup at Hillsborough. There was a copper in front of every turnstile and two coppers behind as well. We must have walked at least six miles in our search for a jibbable entrance before we found the one stile with no Dibble guarding it. We'd passed the same spot umpteen times but, fortunately, this time the coppers were busy nicking other unsuccessful jibbers. We vaulted over like chimps and headed in to watch the game.

Sometimes, jibbing into the ground could cause untold mayhem. One game in the 1974/75 season is a perfect example of this: the bubble blowers of West Ham had been waiting to have a go at us since 1967, when United were crowned the champions of England and overran them both on and off the pitch. This left their hooligans determined to even up the score and, on the day of the match, there was a tangible sense of foreboding. It was a full house and thousands were locked out, but that was easily remedied because some of us vaulted the stiles and others went under like ferrets. What awaited us on the other side was akin to a lion's den. We were immediately battered from every angle by an army of rival fans.

The situation seemed hopeless. What we needed was divine intervention: a fucking miracle. Well, God helps those who help themselves and, as luck would have it, we heard the United lot singing outside our section of the ground. Three of us went up to the big wooden gates that were keeping them out and, peering outside, we saw the Wythenshawe lot.

'Lift the gates!' I shouted. 'Try and get them off the hinges.'

The rest of the lads all shouted similar things and the gates eventually came crashing down as the United lot came crashing in. The cavalry had arrived.

The extra numbers coming into an already packed terrace caused people to flee the crush by jumping over the perimeter onto the pitch. Unbeknown to most, that was one of the main reasons the game had to be halted for 20 minutes. It only started up again when the cops restored some semblance of order. My thoughts that day were, We win some, we lose some, but we always have a go. We got a bit of a beating off West Ham, but I was happy to get home with mind and body intact.

We got up to all kinds of things at the football. One of the most memorable matches I can recall was a home game in the 70s against Leeds. A few of us decided to meet at Victoria train station, where most Leeds fans would be arriving later that day. We met up early doors, hoping to pick off anyone who turned up before the main body of away supporters. We had two very young Salford lads with us who couldn't have been any older than 13. The youngest of these was four foot-odd, but had a massive German Shepherd with him that he'd nicked from a dog's home. It was old and covered in scars but, unbeknown to the lad at the time, it was also a highly trained ex-police dog.

After a while we spied a dozen or so Leeds lads walking brazenly up the ramp inside the station, all wearing their colours. What happened next will live forever in my memory and has given me many belly laughs over the years. The young Salford kid gave his dog the command to attack – and attack it did! In the blink of an eye the beast got two of the rival fans on the floor, causing a third to flee in horror as his coat was ripped from his back. We couldn't stand up for laughing. The shock on those Yorkie faces lives with me to this day It was as funny as it gets.

The British Transport Police went apeshit as we legged it up towards Market Street. They commandeered a taxi and managed to catch up with the little Salford lad, bundling him into the cab and nicking him. They then headed back to Victoria station as the dog went mental because it'd been separated from its master. My abiding memory of the incident is the dog chasing the taxi all the way back to the station. I'm sure those Yorkies must still be having nightmares about their unique welcome to Manchester.

I carried on getting up to no good at the games for the next two years. Some firms would go to games tooled up but we always went unarmed, apart from one game against Newcastle where we felt we needed to even up the odds. This was because we had gone there before and got hammered by the Geordies, who were all big, burly blokes. Luckily, we managed to get the best of them without using our weapons.

After a while, my antics at the matches started getting me into trouble with the police, which my family were none too pleased about. My dad believed in Purgatory and told me I was going to be spending a lot of time there if I didn't change my ways. Mam was equally disapproving but still rooted for me in my court cases. I remember one of the first times I was hauled in front of a judge for fighting at a game. A copper had seen me putting my fists up, but my solicitor managed to shed doubt on his statement by claiming I might have been signalling for people to leave it out. Mam was over the moon when I got a 'not guilty' and put the last £14 towards a sheepskin jacket I'd been paying for in instalments. Sheepskins meant something back then, a real status symbol, so I was absolutely buzzing.

Although they always remained supportive, my parents made it abundantly clear that they hated what I did. One time my neighbours were on their way back from a holiday when they saw me mugging an older lad at Victoria station in London. They told my mam and dad what I'd done and I was dragged out of the house by my ear. I was forced to enrol as an altar boy at church, in the hope that it would straighten me out. It didn't work though, because I managed to fuck it off and went round my mate's house to play three-card brag instead.

Robbing rival lads at the football was quite a popular activity back then. If we saw a young lad wearing a sheepskin, we were having it. Sheepskins were the crème de la crème of terrace fashion. If you had one of those things on your back then you were somebody. Sometimes we didn't even need to take the jackets by force. One time we were at a night game between Man City and Middlesbrough when we saw a Boro fan with one on and started eyeballing him. We saw the fear in the fella's eyes so we made him an offer.

HOTSHOT

'We'll get you back to your coach but you've got to give us your sheepskin,' one of the boys told him.

The maze of alleyways around City's ground was forbidding enough for a native Mancunian, so fuck knows what it must have been like for somebody from out of town. I knew what the answer was going to be before he even moved his lips.

'Sure, no problem,' the geezer told us. 'Just make sure that I get there okay.'

We stuck to our word and walked him to his coach. To my amazement, the moment we got there he started taking off his jacket. He only needed to hop onto the coach and he'd be home and dry without having to hand it over. Fuck knows what was going through the silly bugger's head!

The Boro supporter got off lightly because some fans had their jackets taken by force. George Lyons once followed a Scouser all the way to Salford because he clocked that he was wearing a sheepskin. The poor fella was just crossing the swing bridge over the Manchester ship canal when George pounced on him and ripped the jacket off.

'You can keep the sheepskin,' said the Mickey, resigning himself to the fact that he'd been taxed. 'But can I have my keys out of the pocket?'

'You want them?' smiled George. 'Then you can swim for them, you dirty Scouse bastard!'

And with that he threw them into the water, where they sank without a trace.

It was very rare that anybody would get their belongings back once they'd been taken. Certain items were seen as souvenirs of a game. If you got a rival's scarf it was the equivalent to bringing back a scalp. Almost everyone in our gang would usually return with one after each match. We could have filled a room with all the captured scarves we stole from opposing supporters.

My crazy antics went on until the winter of '76, when my mam got sick of all the court cases and told me she was going to kick me out if I went to any more matches. 'You will not live in this house if you continue to do what you're doing,' she warned me.

I honoured Mam's wishes and stopped going to the games.

Luckily, my older sister was a lot less of a handful. She went to Adelphi House, which was the top girls' school in Salford, and hung around in the mill and mine town of Leigh with her best friend Jackie. They were both top lookers and attracted all of the best dancers from the northern soul scene.

As well as being smart, Jackie also had a very creative side that she channelled into hairdressing. When you got a cut from her, you knew your haircut would look top. I remember when she used a solution that was too weak for my thick, heavy hair and caused my Barnet to fall into a shaggy perm. It looked as if it was meant to be like that and suited me really well, so I guess that even her mistakes worked out for the best.

Jackie was so good with the scissors that she was entered into a national competition in London and got one of the top positions. This was unusual back then because judges in the capital tended to favour their own. It was no surprise to me though, because I knew how talented she was. When she returned home, she was buzzing about her achievement and gave me a new cut to celebrate – and what a cut it turned out to be.

Wow, I thought as I marvelled at the end result. Now that's different.

It was a bit like David Bowie's hairdo but it looked quality on me. This new stylish wedge/flick cut went well with my look, which consisted of Levi's I'd nicked from the Scan supermarket in Walkden, Adidas or burgundy royals with crepe soles and heels, lamb's wool jumpers and white polos from Marks and Sparks (also half-inched). To me, Perry polos were for skinheads, suedeheads and West Ham fans, so I thought, Fuck that, and steered well clear of them. The Levi's had press-studded flaps on the back pockets and a bit of width at the bottom. They were certainly not skin-tight shit-stoppers.

245

HOTSHOT

I'd always been ahead of the curve fashion-wise, because I used to bunk off school to work at the underground market. We had one of the best clothes stalls in the place and I got paid in clobber as well as cash, which meant I always had on all the latest gear. It was a buzz to wear things other people had yet to get onto. At that age, clothes were of the utmost importance and gave us kudos amongst our mates.

Feeling fab with my stylish new haircut, I set off to Leigh to see my girlfriend. I was certain that nobody I knew had seen a look as cool and different as mine before, so I boarded the bus with a sense of confidence bordering on arrogance. The reflection of my Barnet caught my gaze in the window and I started eagerly anticipating the appreciation I'd get. Then I heard somebody shout, 'Who do you think you are? Have you turned fucking queer? Fuck off, you poof!' It wasn't exactly the type of reception I'd expected.

As if that wasn't bad enough, a coach load of amateur rugby players pulled up next to me. They pointed at my head and laughed as they filed past to go to a nearby pub. The worst thing was that I knew most of them; I'd played both with and against them as a scrum-half back when I was a kid.

Word soon got out that I was 'odd' and there was more than one occasion when I came to blows over it. Some of the guys that gave me grief were tough, which meant I often ended up copping for it. One bloke, famous for being handy with his fists, decked me good and proper from one side of the road to the other. He then gave me the same again as I got up to have another go. Realising the futility of fighting back, I shouted abuse at him instead.

'You know fuck-all in your one horse town!' I yelled.

The piss-taking that I received was relentless. On a scale of one to ten, you would have needed more than your fingers and your toes to show how bad it was. I needed to readdress this situation. What to do? As an experienced Red Army lad, I'd learned that the only way to react when your back is up against the wall is to go forward, through your opposition. I still had a lot of self-belief so I took my hair a stage further and got a henna rinse. In for a penny, in for a pound! Those mill town boys didn't know what had hit them.

For a guy with a so-called girly haircut, I received more than my fair share of female attention. It put me in mind of a story I'd heard about when the Cockney Ziggy Stardust first told his rough-arsed northern band, the Spiders From Mars, that they had to go glam. They responded at first with an abrupt 'fuck off'; but when they found out what a hit it made them with the ladies, everyone was slapping the makeup on like there was no tomorrow.

As well as being bang into my fashion, I was also into bands, books and concerts. I discovered my heaven courtesy of an ex-Red Army barmy called Mad Mick, who rolled up a spliff and helped music to become my passion. I fuelled his love of bands as he did mine and we were always sharing new groups that we got onto. He was a big music head and we were both thirsty for culture, so we went to a variety of different gigs together. That guy was definitely a kindred spirit at that moment in time.

But I decided I needed another fix of football in January '78 and went to see United play Carlisle in a cup match. A couple of lads who I'd once stood strong with ridiculed my haircut, which made me feel very uncomfortable, so I went back home to listen to Talking Heads and smoke a spliff instead, as music now occupied a prominent place within my life.

'You look like a girl. Why've you had your hair cut like that? And you've fucking dyed it too!' the boys had mocked me. The funny thing was that it wouldn't be long before they all had 'odd' haircuts as well.

Whenever I was strolling around Manny, it always seemed as if every man and his dog was looking me over. I sometimes felt as if I was either paranoid or hallucinating. One time I told my missus how I was feeling and she confirmed I wasn't imagining it. Occasionally, guys would enquire as to where I'd had my Barnet cut. A change was occurring; people were finally catching on to my haircut. Soon it *would no longer be an oddity; it would become part of a cultural trend that is still talked about today.*

We were originally labelled as 'townies', the subculture that later gave rise to the Perry boys – although I was no longer a match-going Red by that stage. To be honest, I hadn't even heard the phrase until recently, which is strange because I was amongst the first wave. We didn't feel the need to call ourselves anything; we were just game kids who were into our fashion. Whether it was fighting or clobber, us lads were always right up there and laid the foundation for everything that came after.

27
Demon Drink and Drugs

Although my football ban became a positive thing – in that it gave me more time to hear about the experiences of lads like Pev – it also meant I spent more time down the boozer, getting off my rocker. Being pissed and coked up all the time had started out as fun, but by this stage, I was beginning to go a little bit overboard with it. There comes a point where alcohol and cocaine become a part of your lifestyle you are unable to do without. I was never what I'd call an alcoholic or an addict; I always drank and took drugs socially – I just drank too much and took too many drugs. The coke came with the beer. Every time I had a pint, I found myself wanting a couple of lines to go with it. A little dabble soon turned into a gram and, before I knew it, I was off to buy another bag.

At age 30, I split up with my missus and my drinking really spiralled out of control. I partied even harder than before and it soon got to the point where I needed three cans before work and ten throughout the day. If I didn't drink, I felt as if somebody was strangling me, and broke out into a cold sweat. Sometimes I would hallucinate as well. The blinds in my bedroom would look as if they were coming in at me and the patterns on the wallpaper would move about. The minute I got a couple of tins down my neck, I was alright again.

I ended up losing so many jobs through partying that it was unreal. Sometimes I would turn up looking rough as fuck after a night on the tiles; more often than not, I fucked work off instead. My most common excuses were, 'I had a dodgy kebab last night,' or, 'The bus hasn't turned up.' There are only so many times you can use the same blags though, so I had to be creative. One time I told them I'd taken a load of Viagra and still had a hard-on. Nobody was going to question an excuse like that.

I never knew when my benders would come to an end. One Christmas, I went for a pint in Newton Heath and ended up staying there for four years. I'd only intended to have a couple of drinks but I didn't feel like going home. I guess I wanted to show the locals that Hotshot is for life, not just for Christmas.

After a few beers and a bit of Charlie, we would occasionally go round someone's house and finish the night off with some harder stuff. I would smoke crack if it was on offer but stayed clear of heroin. It was a good thing really, because a lot of people don't know when to stop with that shit and it takes over their lives.

Martin went the other way and ended up hooked on gear. The lads would tell him to go easy on the drugs but, at the end of the day, nobody could make the decision for him. Whenever I said anything to him, he reminded me I was in no position to talk, what with my own excessive partying. It was up to him to realise that he had a problem and to try and get clean. Every other week I got a letter saying he had been banged up. I never asked what he'd done but always knew that it was drug-related. He was still my best mate though, so I was always there for him.

I soon realised what a waste of money crack was and decided to fuck it off. I should have done the same with booze but it was too ingrained in my lifestyle. The pub was where I went to socialise; it was part of my daily ritual. Quitting would mean changing my entire routine overnight, which really wasn't about to happen.

My body didn't want me to quit either. I was walking down the street one day, after taking it easy for a while, when I collapsed from alcohol withdrawal. One minute I was right as rain, the next thing I knew I was in hospital with a drip in my arm. The nurse explained that people with drink dependencies run the risk of a seizure if they try and suddenly knock it on the head. I had been taking it a bit too easy and my insides couldn't cope with sobriety.

Just as I thought things couldn't get any worse, a lad called Chris the Book blagged his way onto the ward at two o'clock in the morning by claiming he was my brother. We called him that because he always carried a book with him in case he needed to make a Millwall brick out of something. He was completely off his face and tooled up with a paperback, which was the last thing I needed after nearly dying. I can laugh about it now, but at the time it really sent me west.

I eventually got rid of Chris and managed to recover from my seizure, no thanks to his surprise visit. As I left the hospital, I made a promise to myself to calm down on the drink for the sake of my health. I didn't want to pickle my liver before I reached my fortieth birthday. My fit had been a wake-up call; it was time for me to moderate my partying.

I started cutting down on my boozing straight away. I won't pretend that it was easy, because sitting there drinking orange juice really isn't the same as supping a pint. The other lads were supportive of what I was trying to do though, especially Martin, who was always full of encouragement. By this stage he'd managed to stay off gear for a full year, so he knew what I was going through.

'You're doing great,' he told me one day as I sat and drank my non-alcoholic beverage at a Gorton boozer. 'Make sure you stay on that. I'm just off to sort a babysitter out for my missus' kids. I'll be back in a bit.'

That was the last time I saw him alive. Two minutes later, Robert came running into the pub, shouting, 'Our kid's in trouble!' I followed him out of the door and round to a nearby street, where I saw Martin lying in a crumpled heap on the floor. I knew that he was dying from the amount of blood gushing out of his body. It was literally flowing down the road. Words can't even begin to describe the pain of seeing your best friend bleeding to death. It was absolutely horrendous.

I don't know the exact events leading up to Martin's murder, but from what I've heard he got into an argument with some kids and one of them pulled a blade on him. Martin wouldn't have run away so, as far as I'm concerned, he died because he was game. He was like a brother to me; I could have been his twin. A part of me died with him that day.

One of the locals was eventually jailed for the killing after the police found a bloodstained top at his address. He was caught in Wythenshawe after a high-speed chase and sentenced to a minimum of 23 years in prison. His brother was also accused of taking part in the attack but got a 'not guilty' verdict. He still ended up going to jail though, because the Old Bill found a load of guns and some ammunition while investigating the case and managed to prove that they belonged to him.

'Martin was a decent bloke,' a resident of Gorton told the *Manchester Evening News*. 'He was a regular guy. It's really tragic.'

He was more than just a 'regular guy' though; he was one of the funniest people I ever met in my life. Nobody could crack me up like Martin could.

The whole experience almost fucking killed me. I still have flashbacks of his death and break down when talking about it. Every day I think about the things we did as kids and wonder how it came to this.

Rest in peace, Martin. I know you're looking down on me.

The rest of the community in Gorton was equally cut up. There must have been over a thousand people at the funeral, including a good turnout from the Red Army. The locals did a lot of fundraising so we were able to give him a decent send-off. I've got a lad called Tricky Ricky to thank for that, because he helped to raise a lot of cash.

One of the boys wrote an article about Martin in *United We Stand* shortly after the wake. I think it sums up what he meant to us quite well:

> On the evening of Friday, 23 July [2010], a stone's throw away from where he had grown up in Gorton, Martin Gallagher was stabbed and killed as he walked home with his girlfriend. An innocent victim, Martin was 37 years old when he became the first of three people to lose their life in a similar way on a shameful weekend for Manchester. Martin was a well-known United lad all his life and his loss has been felt hard amongst his family and friends, but most of all by his identical twin, Robert.
>
> Martin was no angel by any means but that was also a reason why he was loved so much by all who knew him. He was a 'funny as fuck' lad with a merciless sense of humour. Even during his dark days spent at Her Majesty's pleasure, he would only ever see the positive side of what was going on around him. This included him taking great pleasure at being 'padded up' with a footballer's brother and educating him as to what was going on off the field whilst his famous brother was on it.
>
> Martin and Robert started going to games in the mid-80s and were part of a new breed of young lads to follow in the footsteps of the Red Army generation. The Inter City Jibbers, or 'Serious Damage', as they jokingly called themselves, became a tight bunch, with

only a select 50 or so recognising these tags even today. This group of lads, mainly from Gorton, Longsight and Hulme plus a few other stray kids from Whitefield, Chadderton, Droylsden and Guide Bridge, made up the bunch following United pre-glory days, together with a young London contingent.

Although Martin was a tough kid, he will be remembered in that group for his loyalty, bravery, humour and friendship. He showed qualities that seem to have been lost with many kids these days from similar backgrounds. It is ironic that many of this group were together the day before Martin died at the funeral of another well loved United lad, Bobby Derek.

On April 4, 1988, all the talk around the packed stand was of United being in the Kop at Anfield and that the 'cheeky Manc cunts' were going to get a pasting. As the match was about to get underway, a denim-dungaree clad Martin Gallagher was seen to make his way through the crowd towards the foot of the Kop, along with a small entourage, all of whom would have struggled buying a packet of cigs, never mind get served in a boozer.

The rumours going round Anfield would prove to be correct and as Bryan Robson opened the scoring, a melee ensued as hordes of Mickeys piled forward, trying to get to the celebrating pocket of Mancs in the Scouse holiest of holies. This is no Danny Dyer-esque thug story where the Mancunian equivalent of Fagin's gang fought off 10,000 Mickeys. Most were escorted out and along the pitch to the away section along with a few cuts and bruises but the fact that they were there at all was piss-take enough.

As the fracas died down, a group of Mickeys at the

scene were pointing out young Gallagher as he was pitch-side, with one heard to say, 'I fucking knew that cunt was in here!' This was not a one-off story. In the late 80s and early 90s, there were not many football firms who didn't know of the Gallaghers from United. The sight of the mixed-race identical twins at an away trip meant that somewhere in the shadows, United had a mob out for business. On moody trips such as a mid-week visit to Spurs, they were a very welcome sight.

Martin and Robert were known to all simply as 'the Galleys', mainly because no one could tell them apart. As schoolboys they began following United and quickly showed they were as 'game' as they come, which commanded healthy respect in a world where many of their peers had a good ten to 15 years on them. The term 'loveable rogue' could have been invented for these lads. They were famous for setting off to away games with a fiver in their pocket only to return with upwards of a score, having not paid for a tap all day. The philosophy of 'to pay is to fail' was more of a necessity and they would get to games and live the life by whatever means they could. If this meant a wallet or contents of a shop till going astray along the way then so be it. Sure they were rogues but they were our rogues.

Losing Martin in such a way is hard to accept but the twins are part of United's off-the-field history and Martin would be happy knowing that he was thought of in such a way. He was much loved and respected. To all that knew him, that is how he will be remembered.

Never were truer words spoken. Martin was my right-hand man. We did everything together and I still feel as if he has my back today. Wherever he is, I know that he will be looking down on the lads and smiling as he remembers all the times we had together. Friends like him come once in a lifetime. It's just a shame that he had such a short time on this earth.

28
The Youth of Today

Me, Martin and Robert might have been regarded as United's younger firm when I was on the scene, but we were by no means the last generation of Red Devil hooligans to wage war on the terraces. One of the best-known youth mobs of the last decade is the Moston Rats from the north of the city. They got their name from the Lancashire Old Bill, who boxed them in at an away game against Blackburn and noted that they were all coked up, pissed and stoned, and none of them had tickets.

'Fuck me,' said one of the officers. 'I've never seen a pack of rats like this before in my life.'

In October 2009, the Rats made headlines for allegedly looting a food kiosk and cleaning out the tills at a Carling Cup fourth-round game against Barnsley, which prompted the papers to speculate that they were the most destructive United firm of all time. 'The Moston Rats have become a source of concern for more experienced United fans who follow the club home and away,' wrote a reporter for *The Independent* shortly after the incident. 'Even by the occasionally wayward standards of the club's fans in the 1970s and 1980s, this latest phenomenon are thought to be the worst yet.'

Others remained more doubtful of the Rats' involvement. 'It was common knowledge by those "in-the-know" that the "Moston Rats" were a group of around 20 teenagers from Moston in North Manchester who had been involved in incidents of disorder between 1997 and 2001, but who were now in their late 20s and on the whole no longer attended matches,' sociologist Dr Geoff Pearson of the University of

Liverpool pointed out in 'A Commentary on "Little Hooliganz: The Inside Story of Glamorous Lads, Football Hooligans and Post-Subculturalism" by Professor Steve Redhead' (published in *Entertainment and Sports Law Journal 8*, 2010). 'There was no doubt that the teenagers who had been involved in the disorder in question were not the "Rats" and were not even from Moston.'

Whether you choose to believe *The Independent's* account or Dr Pearson's, the Rats, who actually number 50, not 20, have definitely left their mark. YL is a friend of the group and of United's younger lads in general:

YL

The Rats are a firm made up of lads from Moston and Miles Platting. They're a game set of lads who always want it and don't take shit off anyone. Their name came about because they're similar to rats in the way they swarm together. All of United's younger lads come together like that as well though, because we're like one big, tight-knit family.

I first got into going to the football through being at school in Blackley with a lot of other United fans. I started watching the matches with lads from Blackley, Crumpsall and Cheetham Hill because these were the main areas that the pupils in the school came from. When I was 17, I got into a ruck with grown men twice my age at a home game against Burnley. I enjoyed the feeling of knowing that the rest of the firm had my back. Me and my mates have been involved in a lot of other incidents since then but don't go to games specifically to look for trouble. We're just always about and if people want it then they can get it from us.

City are obviously one of our main rivals and Liverpool and Leeds both have a major hatred of United. Then there's Stoke, who have picked us as their enemies because they haven't really got a proper rival, and Bolton, who are the worst for giving it all that Munich shite.

The Youth of Today

We get a lot of trouble abroad too, the worst place we have travelled to being Rome. That place is so full of corruption it's unreal. When we went there for the Champions League final, we tried to get a taxi to the Stadio Olimpico and the driver pretended not to understand what we were saying. I gave him 20 Euros and he suddenly spoke perfect English but took us down a back street and let us out in a housing estate full of local hooligans. Hordes of ballied-up Italian thugs were waving knives and throwing bricks at us.

The coppers in Rome put the Old Bill here to shame in terms of corruption. Some of the ones we saw were wearing the badges of our rival team's Ultras. The locals love their weapons over there as well. Some people carry knives in England but round those parts it's commonplace. I don't personally think it's right for hooligans to use blades because I've seen knife injuries before and they aren't what it's all about.

Hooliganism might be thriving in Italy but a lot of lads here in Manchester have been given banning orders and the police are cracking down on us, because United are top of the league for arrests at games. It's harder for our generation than it was for Hotshot's because of all the surveillance and advances in technology, but hooliganism definitely still exists. United's lads have got their heads screwed on and know when to do certain things and when to keep a low profile. Violence at the football will never stop and the Reds will never die.

29
The End of an Era

In a way I'm glad the current youth are carrying things on. Going to the football gave me a sense of camaraderie that can never be replaced. United were like one big family and still are to this day. Nothing can compare to the thrill of invading somebody else's city centre with a big group of your mates. It was a top buzz from day one and I would do it all again, given half a chance.

Nowadays, everything is far more on top with the Old Bill though. There are rules for everything: you can't even stand up and yell, 'Fuck off!' without the Dibble getting onto you. In our day, you could have 10,000 supporters travelling to a city for a match but that would never happen now, because the police can turn you back and send you home for not having a ticket.

The stricter measures that have been brought in make it a lot harder for the new generation of Red Devils to do their thing. Back when I started out, the police would whack you with their truncheons and send you on your way, but the Dibble of today hand out criminal charges as if they were sweets. You only have to look at somebody the wrong way and you can end up doing time.

Despite the authorities' war on lads like us, hooliganism is still going strong. It has existed for as long as the game itself and isn't likely to be eradicated anytime soon. Rivalry and hatred are part and parcel of football. They are what make it so exciting. Without the likes of the Red Army, there would be no edge to the game.

HOTSHOT

There is a bad side to football culture though, because I've lost over 20 mates through drugs, drink and suicide throughout the years. The excessive lifestyle that comes with being a lad is not without its hazards. Quite a few of my friends have died before they reached the age of 40. Then there's the aggro I get off rival firms; I get more trouble now that I'm not looking for it than I did when I was a thug. Lads are always trying to have a pop at me when I'm drinking in town, which is a proper pain in the arse. They never do it when they're on their own either; there are always at least five of them there, trying to put my reputation to the test.

There are also those who think that hooligans are the scum of the earth and give us gyp for it. What they fail to realise is that United didn't go to the games to kick off on innocent people; the violence was always lad-on-lad. We never brought it to anybody who wasn't up for it.

Whether you agree or disagree with the way we lived our lives, we were an important part of our team's history. Without us, other firms would have seen United as an easy touch. We defended the honour of our club and showed our rivals that they couldn't take liberties with the Red Devils.

I wrote this book to reflect on all the times we had together rather than to glorify them. Hooligans are like the mods and rockers: we're a much-maligned subculture that the media has never truly understood.

The Red Devils were brought together by love of our team and would have done anything for them. If loving my club is a crime then I'm as guilty as can be. I was willing to fight to the death for them and still am, to this day. Although I am no longer a hooligan, I will have United in my heart until the end of time. We are the pride of Europe, the cock of the North, and always will be.

A Beginner's Guide to Manc

Rather than changing the way we speak, we have written this book using the language of the city we were born and raised in. Those of you who aren't from round these parts might want to familiarise yourselves with the lingo. Here is a quick rundown of some of the words and phrases that non-Mancunians might not understand ...

Approvey – approved school
Arnie – purse
Ballied up – wearing a balaclava
Ballooning – being loud
Bang off – good
Barmy/shirter – football fan who isn't a hooligan
Battle cruiser/watering hole – pub
Beer monster – somebody who always wants to stay in the pub
Blag – armed robbery
Blocking/chalking – distracting someone so that somebody else can pick their pocket
Boat race – face
Blue-conk/bluenose – Man City supporter
Blues – all-night party in a flat or house
Box of toys – boys
Brief – solicitor or ticket
Bubble – give information to the police
Canteen – prison shop
Chiv – knife

HOTSHOT

Claire Rayners – trainers
Claret – blood
Collyhurst Cowboy – somebody from Collyhurst in northeast Manchester
Cucumbers – numbers
Currant – son (currant bun = son). Also *The Sun* newspaper.
Dan Dares – flares
Dibble – policeman (Officer Dibble was the name of the policeman in *Top Cat*)
Dipping/zapping – picking pockets
Firm/mob – gang
Five-O – police, as in *Hawaii Five-O*
Gerannie – purse
Game – up for a fight or stealing something (from 'gamecock', a rooster specifically bred for fighting)
Gear – heroin
Goon – idiot
Grafter – professional criminal
Half-inched – stolen (pinched)
Hammers – fists
Hector – ticket inspector
Jack – till (Jack and Jill = till)
Jam tart – heart
Jekyll – fake (Jekyll and Hyde = snide)
Jib – avoid paying for something
Jib off – leave
Jolly – someone posh/in a suit
Jump – shop counter
Kipper – face (kipper and plaice = face)
Lad – hooligan
Lifed off – given a life sentence
Little fellas – Ecstasy pills
Long 'un – £100

A Beginner's Guide to Manc

Manor – area
Mars Bar – scar
Mickey – Scouse (Mickey Mouse = Scouse)
Millwall brick – makeshift baton made from a tightly wound
newspaper
The Moss – Moss Side
Munich – derogatory term for a Red
Napper – head
Newton Heaths – teeth
Night boat to Cairo – giro
OB/Old Bill – police
On your toes – running away
Padded up – sharing a prison cell
Persian rugs – drugs
Peter – safe
Pot – drinking glass
Potted – hit with a glass
Rag-arsed – rough
Rattler – train
Read and write – fight
Rice – cocaine (rice and barley = Charlie)
Rocking – good
Rogan josh – blowjob (rogan josh = nosh)
Roots – headquarters
Row – fight
Russell Harty – party
Salford dock – sock
Sausage time – sex
Scran – food
The Smoke – London
Sneak-thief – thief or burglar who relies on stealth
Snide – fake
Straight-goer/straight member – law-abiding citizen

HOTSHOT

Stripe – slash mark
Swag – merchandise sold outside a concert or a stadium
Sweaty sock – Scotsman (Sweaty Sock = Jock)
Tax – steal
Thomas Cook – book
Tool – weapon
Tool merchant – somebody overly reliant on weapons
Trips/windowpanes – LSD
Turn bandit – become a police informer
Twirlers – keys
Whistle and flute – toot (of heroin)
Whiz – amphetamine
Woolyback – somebody from the sticks who isn't clued up

Acknowledgements

I would like to say a big thank-you to everybody who I have watched United with over the years and all the lads who contributed to this book: Galley, Coco, Pev, BV, John, J, Corky, Bez, Andy, Darren, Eddie, Urchin Sam, Scarlet, Benny, C, Mark, P-Macc and YL – this means you.

I'd also like to say R.I.P. to all the friends I have lost; you are gone but not forgotten.

This book is dedicated to anybody who has ever travelled to somebody else's town on a match day with a group of loyal mates and given as good as they've got. Those who have done it will know exactly why it merits being written about. Those who have never experienced it will no doubt think that we've gone mad. Whatever your viewpoint, I hope that you've enjoyed reading this account of our exploits as much as we've enjoyed writing it.

My Friend Martin

Life likes to poke you in your eye, forever friends from
years gone by
Brothers in arms stood side by side, with a swagger of
Mancunian pride
Unknown to each other, united we stood, all having
red running through our blood
Only kids we were out to learn and working our way
up the United firm.

It's amazing what life can do, without United I would
never have known you
I was truly blessed to have met you, and trust my luck
there had to be two
Martin and Rob, an identical pair, I mean right down
to the wire wool hair
A pair or rogues and usually trouble, don't get a
complex, 'You ain't seeing double.'

Our times would be spent huddled together, plotting
up and who to leather
Simple lads, no grace or greed, happy with a tinny and
a fiver's weed
Some of our pranks deserved a BAFTA, with the
constant slagging and lots of laughter
Happy days I'm sure you'll agree, You, Rob, me and
four-foot Ste.

As time goes by the less we are, still bonded by blood,
abate it from afar
Our lives do change, we do move on, I never imagined
that you'd be gone

I got the call like a bolt from the blue to tell me how they'd taken you
I'm still confused, it can't be right, you taken from us on that fateful night

My heart now lies heavy and full of sorrow, never to hear 'Jay, can I borrow?'
Giz a cig, or a swig, or next on that, you really were a tapping twat
But that was you, always trouble and with your kid it cost me double!
To have you back I'd gladly pay, to see your face for just for one day.

God help God now you're there, trying to blag Jesus for a few quid spare
I said a prayer, I hope he got it, it was just a warning to watch his wallet
I'll miss you Martin and say it loud, I loved you mate, you made me proud
Now you're gone, life is unfair, but don't worry Bro we'll soon be there.

Jay Clarke

Designed by Alan 'Tays' Taylor